NURSE

**The Story of One Woman's
Effort to Succeed**

by

Margaritte Ivory-Bertram, R. N.

Landfall Press
Dayton, Ohio
1991

Nurse: The Story of One Woman's Effort to
Succeed
by Margaritte Ivory-Bertram, R. N.

ISBN 0-913428-73-6
Library of Congress Catalog Number 91-076356

Dedication

I most sincerely thank my dear parents, Minnie Allen Ivory and Oscar Ivory, for setting the groundwork and giving me the guidance throughout my young years that made it possible for me to see the dream and pursue the most satisfying and rewarding profession of the nurse.

Acknowledgements

My grateful thanks to my long-time friend and classmate Irene Parrish Dowdell, who provided valuable data, encouragement and support in completing this memoir.

Thanks also to D. L. Stewart and Charles Stough, both of the *Dayton Daily News*, for their assistance, their patience and understanding.

To Theressa Hoover, deputy general secretary, Women's Division, United Methodist Church, New York, for her assistance in helping me sort out the pertinent information, for her generous time, and her recommendations.

For their interest and support, thanks also to Dean W. Pulliam, president of The United Methodist Association of Health and Welfare Ministries, Dayton, Ohio and to Louise Morrison of the Trustees Continuing Corporation of The Women's Home Missionary Society of the Methodist Episcopal Church, Cincinnati, Ohio.

Author's Note

A continuing difficult problem for everyone these days, as our race and color seem to change with politically correct speech, is how to refer to ourselves. This is especially difficult for those of my generation. I note that in most reference books of the past one-hundred or so years we are listed as Nationality — American, Race — Negro. Webster describes "Negro" as black-skinned people from Africa; "colored" as not white-skinned and "black" as a person belonging to a dark-skinned race.

Use of "Black" became popular as an aftermath of the civil rights movement and today, of course, African-American is deemed more politically correct in some quarters.

So we have gone from Negro to Colored to Black to Afro-American. But many of us remain proud to be American and Negro. Some of our oldest and most reputable organizations — such as the National Association for the Advancement of Colored People and the United Negro College Fund — maintain their identity unchanged.

And so do I.

Foreword

With force and determination to succeed in a medical career, Margaritte Ivory-Bertram relates here the events of her early life in Atlanta, Georgia, a grand and thriving southern city that later became one of the chief industrial cities of America.

She speaks fondly and eloquently of Atlanta as being "one of the most progressive and wonderful cities in which to grow up and to be a part of the fine and most lovable people in the world."

Her fond memories of the metropolitan city even during the 1930s and 1940s boasted of excellent public schools and success with their graduates.

The system had well-qualified, dedicated teachers who were extremely helpful and supportive in providing guidance in goal-setting and other areas that are vital for young people to excel in continuing education.

She felt very strongly that the high schooling she received, together with the unlimited advantages provided by the entire community, were essential to her achievements later as a successful member of the medical profession.

This enabled her to achieve her goal of serving humanity as a trained nurse, and to enjoy extended education, travel and family life.

Margaritte writes of the remarkable experiences she encountered in her efforts to succeed; how she feels the strongest influence was having been a member of an old established family of color in Atlanta, and second, the profound influence her church affiliation had upon her early life.

Minnie Allen Ivory and Oscar W. Ivory, her parents, were hard-working, strongly disciplined and caring persons who shared in their childrens' dreams and aspirations.

Their children constantly were reminded that failure was not necessarily the end. They learned to accept no excuse for failure.

They were encouraged to feel good about themselves regardless of their potential, and to feel good about others.

However, Margaritte encountered during her early life some obstacles that were forever present, such as race relations and financial limitations.

Despite these, and other seemingly insurmountable forces, she was able to overcome the odds and move ahead.

Prodded by the incentive to advance, combined with the cultural forces of the Atlanta community, helped her to identify the problems and succeed, keeping in mind the perspectives before her as door after door opened to her.

In 1937 she was influenced by the work of a group of local southern white women who were members of the Methodist Episcopal Church South (now the United

Methodist Episcopal Church).

These women actively worked to help colored families, especially those who were members of the Colored Methodist Episcopal Church (now the Christian Methodist Episcopal Church), by providing further education, scholarships, clothing and religious education and leadership training.

It was during this time that Margaritte learned about one of the health missions supported by these church women: the Brewster Hospital and School of Nursing founded in Jacksonville, Florida, in 1902 for the training of young colored women to become professional registered nurses.

Determined to further her education following graduation from Booker T. Washington High School in Atlanta, she applied and was accepted by the Florida school. She proceeded with the same vigor and determination to succeed.

After the three-year course of study, she was accepted into the American Red Cross nursing services, and later joined the Army Nurse Corps as an Army nurse.

She served almost four years in the United States and one year in West Africa with the 25th Station Hospital, a member of the first group of black nurses to serve overseas in World War II.

In 1987 Margaritte returned to the hospital and training school for the first time since leaving for the Army in 1941 to attend a reunion.

Many changes had occurred. Of all the buildings that had been there when she first arrived in 1937, only the big, red brick central building still stood. The rest had been replaced with new high-rises that now overlooked the old Brewster grounds.

Margaritte felt good about returning, but she missed the beautiful lawns and flowers that had added such beauty to the old campus.

She thought about her early struggles and how things had changed. She recalled the efforts so long ago of those Atlanta Methodist women and their contributions to her success.

She was happy to be back and grateful for all the wonderful people who had been such a help to her.

Catherine Ivory-Davis
Atlanta, Georgia
August, 1991

Prologue

It is good to be a part of something as noble as nursing, to be a member of a profession whose object is to alleviate pain and suffering, to help those who cannot help themselves.

The origins of modern nursing date back to the Crimean War (1854-1856) which pitted Great Britain and France against Russia. Amid the stark conditions of the battlefields and early hospitals, the nursing profession was founded by a remarkable Englishwoman, Florence Nightingale.

One of the greatest women of the Victorian era, Miss Nightingale came to be called "The Lady With the Lamp" by the British troops. Carrying a lantern, she combed the battlefields in search of the wounded and lighted the dark in her nightly hospital rounds to bring comfort to her patients.

In her trail-blazing effort to provide nursing care for the wounded, she blazed a trail to be followed by millions of other care providers. In developing procedures for the proper planning of care for those in need, she set the pace for future generations of nurses.

After the Crimean War, Miss Nightingale returned to England to teach and work at establishing nursing as a profession. Born in 1820, she died in 1910. Her distinguished values continue to inspire the legions of nurses, young and old, male and female, who today choose to follow in her footsteps.

Their calling, too, is the delivery of services to the sick and wounded; their dedication, too, is service to mankind.

The standards developed successfully by our early predecessors in nurse training, organization, program administration and hospital management, still hold for nursing education today.

The professional nurse must never lose sight of those rich and lasting traditions that have made nursing such a rewarding career.

The history of pride, dignity, love and spirituality have remained part of nursing ever since Florence Nightingale. Those of us fortunate enough to have worked in the service of nursing must forever remember the outstanding individuals who started it all.

Pioneers such as Miss Nightingale gave us much for which to be thankful. The modern nurse continues to focus on the positive, and still stands apart from other health care professionals in her neat, crisp, white uniform. In spite of some recent changes in the dress code, the uniform represents cleanliness and orderliness in body and mind. The nurse remains dignified, loyal and in command of her responsibilities.

Regardless of the area of assignment, the nurse is a teacher of health and welfare.

The nurse often is the hope, inspiration and role model for the young. In the workplace, the nurse is an indispensable part of the health-delivery team.

Early in basic training, I learned these fundamental requirements for being a good nurse:

First, to be honest with oneself;

Second, to widen opportunities for learning tolerance and understanding;

Third, to maintain a sense of humor when things are not going well and to make others happy and relaxed about us, and;

Fourth, always possess and maintain a strong commitment to excellence and purpose.

NURSE

Two views of Brewster Hospital: in the early 1900s (above) and in the late 1930s (below).

BREWSTER HOSPITA
JACKSONVILLE, FLORIDA

CHAPTER ONE

Home Missions

The women of the early Methodist Church in the south were a small group of white matrons who were seriously concerned about all women, and their struggle to succeed in family life.

These women were concerned about the foundations of the American home, their children and those of other mothers, and their total communities. They were so dedicated that as early as 1886 they were able to cut through existing racial barriers and prejudices to develop worthwhile missions.

They were able to influence their husbands and families. Often this included a small circle of people for most men, and many women, of that day believed that women who engaged in such civic endeavors were "out of their place."

But this failed to deter the effort to change the American family situation among the underprivileged and downtrodden.

Towards the end of the 1800s, a movement to im-

17

prove their lot swept the country. Largely religiously inspired, it led to the establishment of most of the nation's hospitals, settlement houses, and major educational and political reforms, many aimed at improving the status of women. During the early years of America, those women who were prominent in their own social circles usually were actively concerned most with the management of their own families.

But a number of Methodist women were able to manage the demands of social and family life and to nurture an abiding love of service, making time to help others who were in need.

It must have been difficult for them to convince their friends, families and neighbors. For in those times, women of social standing were expected to be "ladies of leisure."

But these wonderful, caring ladies were dedicated. They did not let obstacles deter them. Nor did they seek acclaim for their efforts to bring a better life to the women of America, and to change America's culture of the time. Their sweeping efforts launched campaigns to upgrade the living standards of all people.

Their work included help for poor white and colored people in America, as well as support for international missions. They were able to help effectively through an organization known as the Home Mission, founded in 1886. It was also known as the Home Mission Work of the Methodist Episcopal Church, South.

The women began their first denomination-wide home mission work long before the turn of the century, and it continued until 1940, when the crusade came under the authority of the newly-formed Methodist Church. That church was the fruit of a merger of the Methodist Episcopal Church, South, the Methodist Episcopal Church and the Methodist Protestant Church. Earlier, however, specifically at a meeting on May 7, 1886 in Richmond, Virginia, the church's General Conference established the Women's Department of Church Extension.

The new department had two major goals:

First, to raise money for the building and maintenance of churches;

And, second, to oversee and maintain parsonages.

The women immediately accepted the assignment to share responsibility for services to humankind. For it was their tenet to share with other Protestant groups, "that Christian missions should meet the physical and social as well as the spiritual needs of people."

They challenged the viewpoint that "religion should have little or no involvement with social issues."

The women came increasingly to the conviction that all persons, because they were creatures of God, "possessed inherent worth, and the potential for useful moral lives."

In the course of their home mission work, the women became more and more aware of the influence of the social environment on the lives of all people, and lamented the harmful consequences of poor living conditions.

In January, 1892 the first issue of *Our Homes* was published as a periodical. Its first editor was Lucinda B. Helm, whose work in those early issues now forms a part of the archives of the United Methodist Communications Information Service in Nashville, Tennessee.

In 1886 Miss Helm became the general secretary of the church's Women's Department of Church Extension. Through her extensive travels she became convinced of the need for a larger home missionary outreach program. Thus was begun in 1890 with General Conference approval, the Women's Parsonage and Home Mission Society.

John Patrick McDowell, author of the *Social Gospel in the South*, explained the struggle that the women of the southern Methodist Church experienced in seeking to extend God's kingdom in the world. "Although never a majority within their denomination, these women were the means by which the Social Gospel, born in the north, came to southern Methodism," he said.

McDowell writes of the effort of the mission, begun in 1886 under the leadership of Lucinda Helm. He describes the progress of the women's attempts to bring better education, nutrition, housing and medical care to the south's poor whites, blacks and immigrants.

Emphasizing the evolution of these women's attitudes, McDowell traces their development from "ladies beautiful" who condescended to the poor, through their later feelings of respect and tolerance for those whom they sought to help.

In this attitude, and in their work in general, the women were encouraged by a growing phalanx of socially concerned Protestants such as Shailer Mathews and Washington Gladden, who at that time were Social Gospel spokesmen.

The efforts of the women were diverse and far-reaching. Throughout the history of their work, they showed particular concern for family stability. And they fought to eradicate conditions that they considered detrimental to home life, from child labor to the ready availability of alcohol. At the same time they campaigned against lynching, supported the pursuit of world peace, and argued tirelessly for increased authority for women within their own denominations.

One such mission was the Scarritt Bible and Training School, now Scarritt College in Nashville. It was, in fact, the first mission, founded in 1890 in Kansas City, Missouri through the efforts of Belle Bennett and the women's society. It was restablished in the Tennessee capital city in 1924, two years after Miss Bennett's death.

Dr. Nathan Scarritt gave land and funds to aid in founding the school, and its first president was Miss Marcia L. Gibson. She was succeeded in 1918 by Dr. Edward F. Cook, and in 1922 by Dr. J. L. Cunningin.

Another outstanding example was Paine College of Augusta, Georgia. Founded in 1884 by the Colored Methodist Episcopal Church (now the Christian Methodist Church) and the Methodist Episcopal Church, South, its mission was to educate young Negro men and women.

The college was named for Moses U. Paine, a Missouri native and a preacher, who provided $25,000 as an endowment fund.

In 1900 the Home Missions Board received a request from Paine College to build a facility to train colored girls

21

in vocational skills. The Home Missions board turned down the request, pleading a lack of funds. Belle Bennett re-introduced the application in 1901.

Shailer Mathews, a Social Gospel advocate, delivered a stirring sermon at the society's annual meeting. Miss Bennett announced the formation of a program to raise $5,000 for the girls' vocational department at Paine. She donated $500 and before the meeting ended had raised $3,000.

This was the beginning of the first real, organized mission by white women in a southern church. And it was successful, as well as gratifying to the women. Paine College got its building and named it Bennett Hall.

Gammon Theological Seminary was another mission, founded in 1883 in Atlanta, Georgia as a co-operative effort of Bishop Henry W. Warren and the Reverend Elijah Gammon of Batavia, Illinois. Its primary purpose was the training of colored Methodist ministers.

Gammon set up the school as a department of Clark University (then Clark College) and at his death left it a substantial endowment. It later merged with Morehouse College's School of Religion (Baptist), Turner School of Theology (African Methodist Espiscopal) and Phillips School of Theology (Christian Methodist Episcopal) to form the interdenominational Theological Center in Atlanta.

The Women's Mission Board encouraged black women to undertake their own home mission work. "As a home evangelizing force," Tochie MacDowell declared, "we must define more clearly our relation to our colored sisters that live among us."

She believed that "God has placed them in our midst, not from their or our volition, and we must help them to higher ideals of Christian integrity and to righteous living."

The women understood themselves to have a particularly heavy responsibility to improve race relations, and they went about doing good and developing worthwhile missions, so much so that today Paine College continues as a leader in the education of Methodist ministers as well as men and women lay leaders.

Colored men and women graduates of the Methodist Women's missions can be found in today's communities as the result of this early work by the southern Methodist women. No group of Americans has done more to improve race relations, solve and dissolve the race problem, than these devoted and caring women of the south, with the help of their northern sisters.

Clark University in Atlanta, Georgia is another recipient of the beneficence of the Methodist ladies. Clark and Paine are highly recognized co-educational colleges, predominantly black in enrollment, among many that continue to enjoy healthy relationships with the white women of the Methodist Church and the black women of the Christian Methodist Episcopal Church (formerly the Colored ME Church). Their programs ensure continued good works through the years, and support students in need.

Other such missions were established in the areas of education and medical care.

One such effort, in Jacksonville, Florida, after a fire swept the city in 1900, was the establishment of an emergency medical clinic. The fire had destroyed mostly the homes and belongings of colored people.

The Methodist women, through their long years of dedicated service to mankind, and their many outstanding missions, have remained active. Their projects are well managed and function to the service of their communities, providing educational opportunities for colored boys and girls who have the desire to further their education.

CHAPTER TWO

How Brewster Came To Be

The story begins with a picture of Jacksonville as it was in the last decades of the 19th century.

It is described by Miss Harriet Emerson, one of the first missionaries of the Women's Home Missionary Society of the Methodist Episcopal Church, who came to the city in 1886 to found the Society's Boylan Home and school. Later she wrote of conditions there when she first arrived:

"Malarial conditions defied all health requirements; and in addition to poverty and the ignorance of preventive measures, disease was a constant menace threatening the unacclimated worker, and making instruction in health and the care of the sick an important subject in the home and school work."

In an article titled "As It Came to Pass — A Story of Beginning," she wrote:

"The older girls accompanied the teachers in calls on the homes, and entered helpfully into the spirit of 'learning to be missionaries,' as one termed it; mothers' meetings held weekly were notably helpful in changing conditions. During the yellow fever epidemic in 1888 this new work was remarkably preserved from the plague.

"From July to December, Mrs. Cecelia Emerson, the beloved housemother (of Boylan Home), and six girls lived in the quarantined city and despite orders to leave, regardless of the girls' welfare, Mrs. Emerson refused to do so and courageously maintained her abiding faith in God's preserving care, 'being kept from fear or evil.' None of the family was ill, and the little home was saved to the work."

From this experience, Miss Emerson had come to the "realization that the Negro girl, with her natural nursing ability" should have skilled training, according to *Looking Backward, Thinking Forward*, the Society's 1930 Jubilee History by Stella Wyatt Brummitt.

Accordingly, a nurse training department was started and the first class enrolled in January, 1901. Miss Iowa Benson of Grinnell, Iowa, a registered nurse from Bellevue Hospital in New York City, was the first instructor. According to the history, the white uniforms and newly arranged classroom created great enthusiasm.

The Jubilee History also reports that about this time Mrs. George A. Brewster of Danielson, Connecticut had been a guest in Boylan Home.

She was especially interested in the helpful phases of the relief work there, and just before returning to her

Connecticut home decided to help.

She said, "I have always been frugal, and should choose to be, since a minister's wife on a small salary has no choice. And since my husband's death I have wished I might be able to leave even a small gift that should be doing good when I am gone. Thinking of places where a little help now would help most, I believe it is right here."

Mrs. Brewster's memorial gift to the Society of $1,000 came like a benediction and soon a sign appeared on a little cottage proclaiming it as "The George A. Brewster School of Nurse Training."

A disastrous fire on Friday, May 3, 1901 nearly destroyed the city of Jacksonville, but miraculously spared the Boylan Home, and it became the relief center for colored victims of the fire.

The fire, according to *The Jacksonville Story*, devastated 466 acres in the heart of the city, destroying 2368 buildings — including twenty-three churches and ten hotels — and left thousands homeless.

Seven persons died in the blaze, which was observed in Savannah, Georgia, 160 miles north. The pall of smoke could be seen 500 miles to the north, in Raleigh, North Carolina.

The indomitable spirit of the community reasserted itself at once, according to the book, with the filing of the first building permit to rebuild on Monday, May 6, when the city reopened.

That same spirit was manifested at Boylan Home. As an "Ark of Refuge" it, in turn, became another opportunity for those caring Methodist women to establish yet

27

another community service by providing for the needs of the many victims of the fire.

Teachers and helpers worked long hours at the Boylan Home, treating many suffering women and children. Since there were no other facilities, they also made thousands of house calls on the sick and injured, helping to distribute barrels of food and clothing. These beginning nurses were of great service in the aftermath of the fire.

As they worked with the injured and the homeless, the women perceived a need beyond providing emergency care for continuing medical services for the black and poor.

They established a treatment unit in a small, one-room cottage on Lee Street. Equipment consisted of one cot, one table and a few chairs. This little facility was known as Mercy Cottage.

From these humble beginnings Brewster Hospital, with one of the first training schools for colored nurses, was born. It was hoped the new facility would provide for all medical needs and perhaps provide some religious guidance as well.

The founding women had religious conviction from which came their determination to succeed in their effort. They brooked no discouraging thoughts, and were able to motivate other white women in the community to contribute as well as those colored people who were able to give. They even had influence with their northern Methodist sisters.

During the following year Miss Benson resigned as director of the Brewster nursing school and Mrs. A. E.

Moreland of Ohio was appointed temporary director. Reports of distressing conditions at the county hospital, according to the Jubilee history, "stirred her sympathy," and with her student nurses visited the patients there every week "with beneficial results." She strongly favored hospital methods as the way to wider usefulness.

The spring of 1903 brought a new teacher, the history continues, Miss L. T. Ross, a registered nurse and graduate of the Chicago Training School. Her ambition was to make the school self-sufficient. Friends and local physicians of both races assisted in many ways, and her work resulted in gain in professional reputation throughout Florida.

After she left, the graduate nurses, assisted by a settlement worker, carried on until the appointment of Mrs. Olive Webster, of Sibley Hospital, Washington, D. C., as director.

Up to this time, the work had been connected with Boylan Home School, the history reports. But in 1904 Miss Harriet Emerson, superintendent of Boylan since its beginning in 1886, retired.

During a transition period of several years, new workers braved new duties. The property location had become valuable, but inadequate, and plans were made for its sale and for a new plant. Brewster Hospital, as it had become known by then, was obliged to seek rented quarters. Because of racial prejudice, only land in the most undesirable section of the city could be found and thus Brewster faced the most crucial test to its continued existence.

The Jubilee history recounts that Mrs. D. B. Street,

then the Society's Hospital Bureau Secretary, "never worked so hard for any enterprise as I have for Brewster Hospital." In like service, Mrs. Webster carried the work through a year that "tested body and spirit."

But a providential change in location was effected through the friendship of an old schoolmate in New Hampshire with the founder of the Boylan Home, making it possible to purchase property in a respectable part of the city.

(In October of 1986, Brewster's first location was named a historical site and placed on the register of the Jacksonville Historical Society.)

The new building, even with the addition of a children's ward and a home for nurses, was still barely adequate to meet the growing needs of both the hospital and the community it served. In 1911, Miss Bertha Dean became superintendent and with the help of her associates carried on a ministry of "helpfulness to a class of sufferers hitherto debarred from hospital privileges," according to the history.

By 1930, the urgent need for more room and better facilities became a top priority and qualified it as one of the outstanding projects for the Society's Jubilee Year. When the delegates met in Cincinnati in 1930, the largest single sum from Jubilee funds, $250,000, was awarded for Brewster Hospital expansion and ground was broken that same year.

The Society's new Secretary for Hospitals, Mrs. Robert Stewart, reported that of the $50,000 fund-raising goal which had been allotted to Jacksonville, more than $18,000 was contributed by the colored community. The

Hospital Guild, which had been organized by Miss Dean, raised $1,500.

In 1931, following the move to Jefferson Street, Brewster Hospital was certified as having an average daily capacity of fifty beds. This smallish bed capacity presented some problems for the nursing school, since many states required that nurses train at larger facilities. Brewster overcame this problem by affiliating with other, larger schools.

Additions to the hospital were built during the 1950s and 1960s and Brewster grew to 117 beds. Other additions and new services followed, including a new cafeteria, a communicable disease ward, and service buildings. At its peak in 1964, Brewster Hospital's total daily bed capacity was 163, with twenty-two bassinets, a new pharmacy, a larger staff, chaplain services and a room set aside for prayer.

It also had a full medical staff, an advisory board of directors, and a fully-integrated staff. Brewster's medical staff numbered more than 180 physicians. It was fully accredited by the Joint Commission on Accreditation of Hospitals and was licensed by the Florida State Board of Health.

Brewster was a member of the American Hospital Association, the Florida Hospital Association, the Jacksonville Hospital Council, the Jacksonville Hospital Educational Programs, Inc., and Blue Cross-Blue Shield of Florida.

The decision to move and to expand, made in 1930 in Cincinnati at the Jubilee convention of the Women's Home Missionary Society of the Methodist Episcopal

31

Church, proved the most portentous in Brewster Hospital's history. It was also perhaps most significant for the Home Mission Society in Jacksonville.

The new location was beautiful. The main building was red brick, located at Jefferson and Eighth Streets, and was beautifully landscaped. Inside were modern kitchens, attractive and spacious dining rooms and adequate nurses' quarters and recreation areas. This was the last major move for Brewster Hospital.

The women of the Methodist Home Missionary Society had achieved most of what they envisioned in the early 1900s: to provide good medical care and religious teachings to the colored people of Jacksonville. They succeeded in their intent to develop an affordable, sound nurse-training program that sent qualified nurses into the medical community for more than sixty years.

CHAPTER THREE

Admission To Nursing School

It was a beautiful day, a day I would remember for many years to come. It was the day I arrived at Brewster Hospital School of Nursing to study to become a professional nurse.

It was September 9, 1937, in Jacksonville, Florida.

This was the first day of the beginning of the best years of my life — arriving on the campus in a taxicab from the downtown railroad station, frightened, confused, and somewhat tired in spite of the new experience.

I was pleased with my effort. The apprehension soon was gone, chased from my mind by the beautiful surroundings of the school.

All around the hospital grounds were beautiful sights. The bright red brick buildings, the large and well-kept lawns, the many multi-colored flowers blooming everywhere, everything was breathtaking.

For a moment, I recall, I stood there and enjoyed the beautiful scene. I was glad I was there in this magnificent place. I admired it and the buildings that were going to be my home, where for the next three years I would study to be a nurse.

I had been so interested in the surroundings at the school that I didn't realize what a big step I was undertaking.

I recalled, for the first time since leaving my family in Atlanta, that I was afraid and homesick. I had butterflies in my stomach, and I didn't like the way I felt.

But I knew that if I was to succeed in enrolling in the school of nursing, I would have to grow up quickly and learn to rely on my own abilities and self-confidence.

I was now alone, with none of the family to help me. All doubts and fears would have to diminish and I would have to move alone at my own speed to achieve a lasting and purposeful career. These realizations proved valuable in my adjustment to life away from home. They would be critical to my training through the years.

The separation from my family proved the most difficult adjustment I had to make.

Mine was a large and close-knit family. There were ten children, six girls and four boys — all highly motivated and with strong religious values. Money was generally in short supply, but the family was stable and industrious.

I always felt it was the stability and determination that brought us through; there were certainly no means other than faith and hard work that sustained us. We were determined to succeed and we worked to do so.

Most family activities involved the church, Holsey Temple CME, and our schools, David T. Howard Elementary School and Booker T. Washington Senior High School. For many years there was never a graduating class from either school without an Ivory in it.

Both schools had excellent, dedicated teachers but when there was need for discipline it got immediate attention at home. One such complaint by a Washington High School sewing teacher to my father concerned my failure to cut and sew my white graduation dress and slip. During those years girls were required to sew their white cotton graduation gowns and the boys were required to make their blue graduation jackets.

Although I was encouraged to meet this requirement, I failed to follow through. Ten years later, when I requested my transcript in order to enter college to study public health nursing, I was shocked to learn that Miss Young, the sewing teacher, had given me a "D," the only such grade I ever received, for failing to make the dress and slip.

My father, Oscar Ivory, was employed by the Atlanta Board of Education as a maintenance worker. My mother, Minnie Allen Ivory, was an elementary school teacher; later she also worked as a practical nurse in private homes. The wages were low but steady and we managed.

My eldest sister, Catherine Ivory-Davis, was as great an influence on me as my parents. Catherine was always in charge, even sometimes when my parents were at home!

A strong person, she stood erect, head and shoulders high, and spoke with authority. One always knew what her ideas and plans were because she was that forceful and effective.

I love her dearly; no big sisters could have done more to provide a solid family structure or been a better influence on me and my sisters and brother.

It was a Sunday when I boarded the train to leave home to enroll in nursing school. That was probably the worst possible day of the week to leave home, because eating Sunday dinner was something special in my family. One didn't miss Sunday's dinner at the Ivory house.

Eating together was a treat. This was the time we all sat down and conversed, debated, discussed one's failures as well as accomplishments.

It was a southern tradition, typical of large families. It was a time of togetherness as a loving and caring family, who supported each other. This togetherness was part of our early lives, and this affection was later transferred as we grew, left home, and started families of our own.

I thought of that last Sunday dinner, which I had enjoyed only a few hours before. But I was jolted from the reminiscences by the realization that I was now standing at the door of the Brewster Hospital School of Nursing. I was at the nurses' quarters, requesting admission.

I recall how good it was to be there, in spite of all the fears I had experienced. I was glad to be there, glad to be one of the members of the entering class of 1937, to be accepted by the School of Nursing.

As I observed the beautiful campus, I recalled the things I had heard about the state of Florida. I remembered hearing my father speak about the climate, and the joy of living in Florida.

He often referred to Florida as "the land of the sunshine." Papa often said, "The sunshine, the warmth, the flowers made one feel good to be alive!" He was right. I was already enjoying what he had said about the sunshine state.

Then suddenly the door opened and, once inside the office of the nurses' quarters, I was welcomed by a small, middle-aged white woman dressed as a "deaconess." She introduced herself as Miss Edwards, the house matron. She was cordial, friendly and invited me in. Her friendly approach helped so much, as for a moment I had been feeling those butterflies return to my stomach. However, her smiles soon removed my anxiety and with that out of the way, I was enrolled.

Miss Edwards was a member of the white Methodist Episcopal Church Home Missionary Society.

Since this was the first time I had ever been away from my home, Miss Edwards was helpful and supportive, as she was with each new student. That is one of the advantages of attending a private, small school. They offer more support from the staff which lessens the tension and anxiety. Small schools can provide the homelike environment that is so important in helping new students adjust.

I was told I would be meeting other new students. Eventually I was escorted to the living area that housed incoming student nurses. It was a large open sleeping room with several windows overlooking the back of the campus. I could see many blooming azaleas and roses from those windows.

Coming from this room were peals of laughter, friendliness and joy. This was to be my temporary sleeping room, with all the other incoming students. Several had already arrived, and were rapidly making friends with one another. Like me, they all were pleased and anxious to become friends.

Miss Edwards introduced me to the four new students in the room and suggested that we spend some time becoming better acquainted. We hardly needed her suggestion. I could tell instantly, from the smiles of welcome on their faces, that I had found a place among friends.

The new students were Irene Parrish, from Cincinnati, Ohio; Evelyn Jefferson, from Hazelhurst, Mississippi; Annie Sue Martin, from St. Petersburg, Florida; and Ida Mae Trapp, from Newberry, Florida.

Meeting these four young ladies was the beginning of long and lasting friendships that have remained intact over the years. We continue to stay in touch with each other with interest, concern, support and love among all our families.

During our first hours of friendship we five new colleagues discussed why we had selected the Brewster School of Nursing as our school, despite the availability of other schools of nursing that accepted colored students.

I recall that the feeling was the same among us all. We had selected Brewster, from among other fine schools, for many reasons.

First, the school was highly recommended and academically stable.

Second, it was private, religious, and affordable. This was important to me. Then as now, I relished the security that Brewster Hospital gave me. And this was, after all, the Depression and there was little money for education beyond the public school level. Grants and scholarships were almost non-existent for colored students.

Nursing offered opportunities for many colored students who were academically qualified and financially able to attend nursing school. Graduation from a nursing school was an assurance of steady employment with a good income.

Therefore, we each felt strongly that the acceptance, training and finally the graduation from an acceptable school such as Brewster would certainly provide good job opportunities — and salaries — as well as lead to a satisfying and rewarding profession.

During my discussion with my four new friends I revealed how I was influenced to become a nursing student at Brewster. Many months before, while I was writing letters of inquiry to several nursing schools that admitted colored students, I met Lila Porter. She was a senior nurse from Brewster and was spending her third year as an affiliate student at Grady Hospital, a large general hospital in my hometown of Atlanta.

Lila Porter was a beautiful young lady with a charming personality. She impressed me at once as an ideal person and a promising student. She assured me that I would benefit by attending Brewster. She really influenced me to the point that I immediately contacted Brewster, seeking admission.

Lila Porter's encouragement and praise for her alma

mater reinforced the good things I had heard about the school from my church contacts and were among the most important things that swayed me toward choosing Brewster. Another important consideration was Brewster's entrance and tuition fees — $50.00 to matriculate and $50.00 tuition. At that, I had to work two jobs to raise the money.

I found out later, while attending, that it truly was an excellent school with an outstanding staff and management.

The getting acquainted continued all day. I later met other new students as well as staff people, many of whom would contribute to my schooling at Brewster. As the day went on, my classmates and I grew less and less anxious and tense, and as the new students arrived one by one, we greeted them each as members of a quickly forming new family away from home.

Near the end of the that first day, our class enrollment had reached thirteen. I believe this was the number of students expected in the freshman class of 1937.

After the formal introduction of each student, sleeping arrangements for the first night were made in that large sleeping room and in smaller rooms. We happily found places for our personal things, and were then escorted to the dining room for our first supper in our new home.

It was my first Sunday evening away from home and family. That was the most difficult thing for me to accept. And to make it more difficult, it was also the first time I would eat a supper consisting of cold cuts and applesauce. This was an experience I would never forget

— the Famous Cold Cut Supper that would linger in my mind (and throat) for many years. Meeting the cook didn't help either. We later learned to hate the cook for his famous Sunday dinners and his seeming dislike for new student nurses.

But due to our need for food, we all learned to tolerate the cooking, and learned to like him a bit.

But it really was an effort.

After supper we returned to our sleeping room. I continued to think about the unusual Sunday supper, but what really was on my mind were the dining room facilities. When we had arrived there, I had seen two dining rooms, one for the white staff and the other for the colored staff.

They were the same. Both were beautifully decorated with spotless white linen tablecloths and matching napkins. There were open areas of the dining rooms and softly colored ceiling lights. The furnishings of the two dining areas were identical.

Today, some people would find it difficult to understand the twin dining rooms, for white and colored people. But this was during the 1930s, and segregation of the races was the way of life in America.

I remember looking at the two rooms and thinking, "This is what they mean by separate but equal." Although born and raised in Georgia, and having lived in a completely segregated environment, this was my first real awakening to the double standards of segregation.

Somehow, I had never thought much about the segregated patterns in Atlanta, where I had lived all my life, because all eating establishments there were segregated. A person of color simply did not eat out because of that pattern. I was becoming aware of the situation at last, and I had never seen a completely duplicated "separate but equal" dining place before. It concerned me.

I thought about it for a while, and then I decided that I should not let it bother me too much. After all, I was there at school to learn, and those conditions would somehow resolve themselves in due time.

Returning to the big sleeping room after supper, I began to unpack my big traveling bags.

I had $100 to pay for my tuition. It was the first time I had ever had that much money. I didn't know how to protect it, and I had heard of students who misplaced their money, or lost it.

I was not going to lose mine. I recall putting $50 in one sock and the rest in another sock for safekeeping. At first it seemed the right thing to do, but the more I thought about it, the more it seemed silly and childish. Then I felt ashamed of my suspicion. I returned the money to my purse and was secretly amused by my little scheme.

I had just finished my unpacking and had located my bed when I heard quick footsteps, and a voice informing all new students that it was nearly time for the lights to go off. I looked up, and there was the house matron, Miss Edwards, motioning us to hurry to bed.

This was the second shock I encountered on my first day at nursing school — and this was one that would take some doing to grow accustomed to — someone turning out the lights by the clock. Even with my parents, we always had ample time to study and prepare for bed. I had to keep reminding myself that I was not at home.

I was now a student in training to become a professional nurse. I was aware that I would have to obey the
rules and regulations, no matter how strict they seemed
to be.

Again I thought about the seriousness of schooling
and the need to succeed.

I had two older sisters who had graduated from
outstanding schools of nursing. There was Catherine, my
eldest sister, a graduate of Grady Municipal Hospital in
Atlanta, and Gladys, who was a graduate of Columbia
General Hospital in Columbia, South Carolina.

I knew I could not do less than they had done. And
they were enjoying their work, and encouraging me to
do likewise.

So now, faced with lights out, I hurried about making
preparations for retiring. A few fast comments to my new
friends and I was off to bed.

But before I could sleep I remembered how grateful
and happy I was to be here, and how fortunate I felt to
be one of the members of the incoming class.

Feeling warm and pleased with myself, I soon fell
asleep.

Nurse Ivory in Brewster Hospital's children's ward.

Student nurse Ivory in March, 1938, after probationary period.

CHAPTER FOUR

The Morning After Admission

The morning afterwards was as exciting and fulfilling as the first day of admission.

I recall waking from a good night's sleep and looking out the windows. The scenery was even more beautiful than I had noticed the day before. Among the flower gardens and shrubs I saw a rainbow created by the spray of the water sprinklers.

It was such an impressive landscape that I thought I had stepped into a painting that stretched across the sky. The beautiful sight was nature at its very best. This was Brewster School of Nursing. This was Florida.

The first day began with a full schedule. We had been informed the day before as to when we should report for breakfast. The meal was served in the same formal style as the previous evening's supper.

After breakfast we were escorted to the office of the

hospital superintendent, Clara Kreuger. Each one of us was introduced to her, and we told her what state we were from, and gave a short statement as to why we wanted to be nurses.

She welcomed us and expressed her pleasure to have the members of the class at Brewster. She also said she hoped each of us would apply our knowledge and become successful graduates.

She seemed as pleased as we were to meet one another. She also seemed strong, carefully observing each of us, her tone of speech — with a heavy German accent — held our attention to what she was saying. I observed immediately that she was a forward person. Her eye contact and body movement indicated a firm and businesslike personality who presumably would expect her nurses to be likewise.

In her manner and approach to the incoming students she seemed to indicate she wanted the best students, the best behaved as well as the best academically. In fact, she was quick to say:

"During your education, only the best students academically, morally and physically will be able to complete the three years' study at the School of Nursing because of our comprehensive program."

She made me aware of the need to study and apply what potential I had brought with me.

Following the meeting with the superintendent the new students were taken on a tour of the hospital grounds, including the nurses' quarters.

During the tour we saw much of the interior and exterior of the hospital and grounds. We also met many staff members who would later be our instructors and supervisors on the floors or in the clinics.

The interior of the hospital and the nurses' quarters were as attractive as the outside even though the buildings had been constructed during the early 1930s. The hospital building at that time was three stories tall.

It was quite small in comparison to the big modern hospital structures we have in our cities today.

But I felt good about the building. It was modern, a bright red brick with large, attractive windows and doors that seemed to beckon me, saying, "Welcome!"

My first impression was that the hospital's inside structure was as exciting and interesting as I had found the outside area to be when I had arrived on campus. The hospital buildings and landscape added a prominence to the neighborhood and to the surrounding area, creating a community within a community.

Inside, there were long, wide hallways that connected every floor and every department. These halls sparkled and glittered, showing the superior daily care they received. It was a pleasure merely to enter the building.

Once inside the doorways, the halls conveyed a feeling that the personnel and medical staff here insisted on offering only the best and most complete care possible.

The basement area housed the heating and engineering department, housekeeping facilities, laundry, storage of supplies, the morgue, a beauty salon for student nurses, and the patients' clothing storage room.

We later visited the first and principal floor of the

hospital. Services located on this floor included the information and admitting department, the reception room for families and friends of the hospital, the pharmacy, the library, the laboratory, the kitchens, and the two dining rooms.

Located in the center of the main floor, near the dining rooms, were the superintendent's office and living quarters. Also nearby were the beautifully furnished guest rooms, available for visitors.

On the extreme eastern end of the first floor was an outpatient clinic. It was one of the best operational outpatient clinics in the area for treatment of colored patients.

We were frequently reminded that patients admitted to Brewster Hospital were treated with dignity, courtesy and given quality care at all times.

Everyone associated with Brewster knew this was of primary importance, whoever the patient was or wherever he or she came from. The tour guide, who was a graduate of the training school, was familiar with the total area.

During my early years of training, the orientation period was the most difficult. Suddenly I was involved in classwork, demonstrations, ward, and other assignments that kept me busy during the day.

The first six months of training was a probationary period during which a student nurse was carefully tested academically and observed closely in the areas of nursing arts, spiritual values, personal relationships, health and mental attitudes. Also important was the student's self-esteem and ability to adjust to her total environment.

These first six months were spent almost entirely in the classroom learning about the nursing arts, procedures and techniques of bedside care.

Many hours were devoted to acceptable behavior, attitudes, brotherly love and personal relationships; these were some of the true values expected of nurses. Students considered for graduate professional nursing were carefully selected. At the end of the six-month probation, if they passed, they were "capped" and permitted to continue their studies for another three years.

That was the way it was in all the nursing schools; the schools wanted only the very best to become professional graduate nurses.

It was very important for the students to adjust to the requirements, apply themselves and work to the best of their ability to get through this period. Earning the "capping" was the first and most difficult area of acceptance into professional nursing and not everyone made it, echoing the warning the hospital superintendent had given us during our first visit with her.

The capping ceremony was serious and dignified. With the teaching staff in atendance, each candidate lights a small white candle and upon reciting the Florence Nightingale pledge is accepted as a full-fledged nursing student. She is now ready for limited duty on the wards, giving bedside care.

One of our first assignments was to give afternoon care on the wards. This consisted of a back rub, straightening out the bed sheets, cleaning the bedside tables, putting fresh water in the patient's drinking water pitcher, and offering bedpans and urinals.

It was one of the first clinical duties of a beginning student. Each would be assigned two or three patients and if her clinical functions and techniques were satisfactory she likely would be assigned additional patients. Early ability to accept responsibility as well as proficiency in care-giving were some of the qualities looked for by the teachers.

The first time I was assigned this duty I went to the third floor. This floor housed mostly male patients plus Crippled Children's services; there were also ten private rooms with baths. On the second floor were the operating and delivery rooms, obstetrics and newborn care, and also other services for female patients.

The third floor was supervised by a Brewster graduate, Mrs. Ethel Harris. She was a hard-working and respectable nurse who gave much learning, support, guidance and love to the students.

The first patient assigned to me as a new student was a Mr. Shields, who had been injured on a Works Progress Administration (WPA) job. The WPA, one of President Franklin D. Roosevelt's New Deal agencies, was designed to stimulate U. S. industrial recovery from the Great Depression of the 1930s by pumping federal funds into large scale contstruction projects.

Mr. Shields was now a paraplegic confined to his bed with little or no use of his lower limbs. He required total personal nursing care.

I remember how frightened I was when I walked into the ward of four men and was told that he was my responsibility for evening care.

All of my young courage and eagerness to serve left

me. Again, I wanted to go home. It seemed that going home was forever in my mind when things appeared challenging.

I found it most difficult to give care to a grown man, especially those duties involving bathing or a bedpan. I paused, hesitated, and slowed my once confident walk to a slow one.

This was my first test of courage, and certainly the first time I questioned my readiness, my desire to be a nurse.

I must have shown those feelings because Mr. Shields looked at me hard and long. He was a large man, muscular and tanned, probably from hard work in the Florida sunshine. He flexed his upper limbs but could not move his legs. He spoke loud and clear. His condition was difficult for him to accept, and most likely was the basis for his cross attitude.

He was looking at me as though wondering why the staff had assigned him such a frail, scared student. Finally he spoke to me:

"Don't you think you can take care of me?" he asked.

Immediately I felt less tense and less afraid. I forced a smile.

"Yes, sir," I said, "I can."

And this was the beginning of a long and lasting nurse-patient relationship.

I got over the second worst shock when I had to place him on a bedpan. I knew the procedure from class, but somehow things have a way of not happening on the ward in exactly the same way that they do in class. The patient was helpful; he still had use of his arms. He was proud of his muscular arms and immediately said, "Here, you put the pan there and I'll hoist."

I did that, and placed the toilet paper in his reach, pulled the curtain and advised him to ring the bell when he was finished.

It gave me a chance to get out of the ward and relax. I realized I had experienced the most unpleasant nursing duty that every nurse must confront in her early training. I knew then I had a lot of growing up to do if I was going to be a cool nurse. Thanks to Mr. Shields, I did grow up and learn to master the evening care shift and the bedpan procedure.

There was so much to learn and such a short time in which to learn it all. But I, as a nurse and like all nurses, was expected to do a good job regardless.

Most patients on the wards were treated as medical, surgical, obstetrical or orthopedic cases. Crippled children, referred to Brewster by the Florida Crippled Children Commission, were special and separate from pediatrics. Veneral diseases and out-patient clinics were important departments; mental health services were just beginning.

When we were not on duty on the wards or in classroom assignments, we had little time for recreation, but we made good use of the time we had. My four classmates and I often took evening walks through the parks and worshipped on off-duty Sundays at a church of our choice.

But I can't recall any time, in spite of the long hours of ward duty and classes, when any of us became tired or disheartened. We all worked and studied hard. We had the same desire to follow the school's guidelines and graduate as was expected.

Every one one of us wished with all our energies to become another of the well-trained Brewster nurses, giving excellent bedside care, teaching and demonstrating the highest tradition of quality nursing and instructing in the nursing arts.

During the first and second years of training, we spent long hours learning about all aspects of nursing, including the early history of Florence Nightingale, the founder of modern nursing.

We also studied others who had made contributions to the profession, but one class in particular seemed most meaningful. It was the study of the Brewster Hospital School of Nursing. Just knowing the rich history of this institution brought me closer to the realization of why I had chosen to study here.

After listening to the instructor tell us of Brewster's history, the members of our class were overwhelmed. We could relate to the story. Some of us had contact with Brewster graduates. Some of us were members of the Methodist Church, and were aware of the work carried on by the Women's Missionary Society of the white church.

But most of us were unaware of the rich history of the school. Learning about it reassured us of the type of training to which we would be exposed. We understood why we were expected to succeed and graduate and go out into the medical field as a product of a highly regarded school of nursing — a finished product with a deep sense of spiritual and professional values, good behavior, proper dress and manners at all times, on or off duty.

This was the way it was in the early years of schooling. Only students who were able to meet the strictly-disciplined lifestyle, and to maintain the levels of academic accomplishment, were able to remain in training.

Integrity and the use of values were stressed throughout our training. Many young nursing students did not understand the philosophy of the rules concerning dismissals, but no one dared to speak of disapproval.

I recall that at the end of the history lecture, everyone felt strongly about Brewster and grateful to those wonderful women who saw an opportunity to serve mankind as an aftermath of the 1901 fire. They took a stressful situation and turned it into a noble work, the founding of the hospital and training school.

The founders responded willingly, and in such an unselfish and caring way that their ideas are appreciated and are being followed through the years. Their service began with a single act of kindness — the Mercy Cottage — which lasted more than sixty-four years.

Their service to humanity and desire to promote education and career development for colored women enabled those colored women to elevate themselves and their families while promoting better health and welfare among the sick and shut-in.

Other classes and other instructors were interesting and impressive as well.

One such class was surgical nursing, taught by Matilda Walker, the surgical supervisor. Mrs. Walker was one of the best-loved staff members. She was one of a kind. She was humane, kind, thorough and knowledgeable, highly respected by students, staff doctors, management and everyone associated with Brewster Hospital. Her ideas, advice and knowledge were often sought when decisions needed to be made.

Matilda Walker was an endless influence on us all. When I was assigned to the Army Nurse Corps after graduation, she was one of the first persons to wish me well, and she gave me some wise words on professional behavior.

She also remembered me with greetings while I was on duty in West Africa. Our lives have been made richer by having known and studied and worked with her. I have even referred to her often as "Mrs. Brewster" because she represented so many fine things like Brewster.

There were other teachers important to the student nurses. I recall my Drugs and Solutions class, taught by Dr. Roosevelt F. Mills. Dr. Mills was a tough teacher. You really had to work to get his lessons. He was pleasant, thorough and spent many class hours trying to make me understand this very important subject.

In those years, many drugs came in stock supplies, and dosages had to be figured from stock strength. This was very difficult for me. Once, on an Easter Sunday weekend, I failed one of his exams and was restricted to the nursing school grounds until I corrected the failure. After the restriction, I made a better effort to understand the theory of drugs and solutions. I also remembered Dr. Mills.

One of my first classes was pathology, taught by Dr. Oscar McIntosh. The first assignment he gave us was to write a short paragraph on why we entered training to become nurses. I was eager and ready to state my reasons. I wrote:

"I came into training to give care to the sick and to help *falling humanity*, and to aid in restoring the sick and shut-in."

Dr. McIntosh looked at me hard and long. I'll always remember the expression on his face. As a young, new student I had enthusiasm that he did not want to dampen, but he had to correct me. He waited for a long time, and then slowly said, "Nurse Ivory, I believe you want to change the words 'falling humanity' to something like 'suffering humanity.' "

Of course, I was always ready for corrections. I accepted his advice in stride. But from then on I was always careful not to use that phrase again.

That correction, and others, helped to make my nurse training period rewarding and enjoyable, and later they made my career very successful.

CHAPTER FIVE

The First
Three Years

During the next two years of training I experienced many changes in adjusting to my new way of life.

The most significant was the loosening of strong ties with a family that lived, played and worshipped together. My family was close-knit, strong, caring and sharing, and one doesn't become independent from such a family without some major adjustments.

Second, I learned to understand my strengths and weaknesses, learning to rely on my own judgement. This strengthened me and made me strive even harder to succeed.

During these first two years there were many instances when I needed support. It was always there. By gradually maturing to adulthood in training, I became self-supporting in my process of thinking, and in my behavior.

During those two years of study I found the same love, respect and caring in others as I had known in my immediate family. Slowly I became involved in the nursing arts in the classroom and the wards where I did my bedside assignments.

My favorite classes included nursing history and ethics. My best grades were in pathology, pediatrics, orthopedics, children's diseases and psychology. I was only a fair student in chemistry and biology and I thoroughly disliked obstetrics.

The ward duty was an enjoyable aspect of my training. I always could count on the usual good supervision and directions from the staff. They were magnificent at creating that very important meaningful learning experience for us students. During the first two years much is expected of nursing students, and much was given.

I feel very strongly about this area of training because, from my own experience, I know that the difficult studies and other assignments during the first two years strengthen the student nurse and help her to perfect her performance in her professional responsibilities later.

During my first two years, and throughout training, I had a weight problem. I was about seven pounds underweight, due probably to poor eating habits during childhood. Although we usually ate wholesome foods at home, low income families such as mine sometimes lacked good nutrition and proper meal planning. It had caused me problems even before coming to Brewster. My application for admission had been delayed until I was able to gain the weight proportional to my height.

I ate everything I could, but still it wasn't enough. So

I had bought Brewer's Yeast pills, the only source of Vitamin B that I could afford, and I ate the pills daily. Sometimes they made me so light on my feet that I felt I was flying, and other times I felt heavy. But when I finally weighed myself before admission, I was seven pounds above the minimum limit.

During the first six weeks of training, I was weighed every four weeks. I ate regularly to maintain my proper weight.

The second personal problem I encountered in training was my inability to turn and lift heavy patients. Mr. Shields, the first patient I had for PM care, was a large man and required a lot of care and lifting. It concerned me enough to consult the Nursing Arts instructor, Miss M. Smith. She demonstrated with a teaching doll, which we called "Miss Chase," and showed me how to lift and turn heavy patients without injuring myself.

My small size and lack of strength were continuing problems for me and required constant efforts to overcome. But the help I received with both problems has lasted with me, and even today I make use of my instructors' suggestions to give good, safe nursing care.

Two classes that were very helpful and really necessary were the most beneficial in bedside care. They were Professional Ethics and Bedside Manners.

While other courses were required and equally necessary, these two were the ones that most influenced me, not only as a student but even today.

The objectives of these classes continue to be of extreme value to me in my daily care and supervision of patients. And the truths of those subjects also have been helpful in dealing with other persons, not just patients.

I constantly was reminded during my schooling that the theory and practice of nursing at Brewster were the best. Academic excellence was expected to combine with sound mental and physical health as well as spiritual strength, contributing to our total development of values and wholesome working relationships with the professionals and others, to provide quality care.

Brewster was small in bed capacity, but it offered a thorough nursing program that was gratifying to its nurses after they graduated and went to find exciting opportunities in all areas of nursing. All class work was thorough and based on latest scientific knowledge.

As the first and second years passed, I continued to enjoy the schooling, the nursing arts, care of my patients, meeting new friends, overcoming daily problems, and looking forward to the third and last year of schooling.

For graduation would be one major step toward accomplishing the requirements of the basic diploma. During this time I was feeling much less tense, more relaxed and somewhat grateful that I was able to master some of the most trying and difficult areas of a vocation that required much of a person.

By the time my second year was fairly well along, I was aware that my third and final year would be spent at Grady Hospital in Atlanta. There I would receive additional studies and experiences in other special required areas not offered in the Brewster nursing program. In this large hospital I could gain experience that was not even possible in most classrooms.

Nursing theory and practice I learned in the classroom

were transferred to the bedside of patients, so it was important that we learn them. They would continue to serve as a pattern of care of the sick regardless of the branch of nursing that a graduate chose.

Affiliation was a necessary evil. It had to be done. During the 1930s, Brewster was forced to affiliate its student nurses to other, larger medical centers due to the unavailability of certain courses. These included psychology, psychiatry, pediatrics, advanced nutrition, communicable diseases, and eye, nose and throat.

Brewster's training school was accredited in every area except those. Grady Hospital, a general hospital affiliated with Emory University Medical School, was an excellent place for further study and to pick up those courses needed to complete state and national requirements for full reciprocity anywhere in the country.

It was something of a dilemma for me, but affiliation served its purpose. The standards of the National League of Nurses, as well as state and local nursing organizations, required nursing schools to provide training in these areas to keep their accreditation. Since its opening, Brewster had supported these standards.

My class spent the entire year at Grady. Our experience was broad and interesting and what we learned was valuable. The experience further helped prepare us for graduation.

The idea of leaving my home school in the third year was somewhat discouraging at first, but after arriving and realizing the vast opportunities for study and work at such a large hospital, I quickly saw the advantages.

61

I soon adjusted to the new surroundings and quickly felt comfortable using my knowledge from Brewster. We all felt very grateful to the loyal and dedicated staff at Brewster for having done such a thorough and sound job. This made it easier to fit in with the higher tension of a big institution.

During some of the leisure time I had during my affiliation year, I often thought of those staff members at Brewster. I did so with feelings of gratitude for their contributions to my early years of training.

The night supervisor, Hettie Thompson-Mills, for example. Mrs. Mills was quiet, reassuring, patient, and pleasant. She was also the cleanest and neatest person on duty. She was firm and knowledgeable, but kind and helpful at all times. It was a pleasure to work with her.

Mrs. Mills continues to serve as a true inspiration for all who knew her. She is still active as a community leader, alumna of Brewster and a member of the Community Nurses Association.

There were other staff members I feel were helpful in preparing me for my third year adjustment away from my home school. One such person was Susie Davis.

Susie didn't know it, but she was my role model in training. She was a strong influence on me during my first two years. I am grateful for her time and energy and for the lasting inspiration I received from her. I also worked under the guidance of Marian Moss, another head nurse I deeply admired. From both these wonderful nurses, I learned basic nursing techniques.

As the year ended, I was anxious to return to our home school for graduation.

This was the event for which I had worked, studied, made adjustments, and looked forward to.

I recall the feeling of anticipation, after such a long wait. With joy and pride I had finally reached that milestone in my career, and I looked forward at last to slowing down and relaxing more. I kept thinking, too, what it would be like to have a job, and a salary with which to purchase the things I wanted.

After years on tight budgets we were now anxious to secure employment to earn the money for some of the "good things of life." I recall how happy we were that at last we had completed the most difficult phase of our training.

The next challenge was to take and pass the Florida State Nursing Boards and get that coveted R. N. after our names. In October of 1940 I took the state boards, and passed!

The training had ended, but graduation was the beginning of a career that would ultimately provide me with unlimited opportunities, travel, graduate schooling and a happy family life.

So at the end of my third year, we returned from Grady Hospital to Brewster, for graduation. It was September, 1940.

Brewster Hospital's 1940 graduating class.

CHAPTER SIX

Graduation

Finally, graduation day arrived. It was a day I had worked and struggled for and awaited with great anticipation. I think the others felt the same.

Graduation is something we all remember in our own special way. For me, it was a feeling of completion, of a task begun and ended; a strong desire to improve oneself, and seeing it through to the finish. We never knew for sure during our three years of schooling whether we would be successful at the end. In my situation it was a good ending.

It had been three long years of hard work since I started in search of my dream to become a graduate nurse. Now, with those years behind me, I have had moments to reflect on what really happened in those years of study.

I still remember how impressive was the beauty of the school surroundings on the day I arrived. The bright red brick buildings seemed so clean and inviting to me, and all those blooming multi-colored flowers everywhere, how enchanting the scenery was to me.

But nothing, nothing, in the surroundings of my new home compared with the joy, love and admiration I found on meeting my first four classmates and the warm friendly staff, the patients and friends. These places and people would become history, but the memories of them would remain firmly with me in time to come.

These events would be a source of much joy and happiness to me throughout my life and would inspire me to continue in my profession of service to humankind.

After graduation, I seemed to have an even greater purpose to serve. Studies and work no longer were the hard burdens they had seemed when I was a student. It seemed that I had found a new purpose — to promote good care for the sick. Graduation has a way of relieving that stress and discomfort and I was experiencing a new freedom to go and take part in a noble and necessary profession.

I felt that graduation was a part of growing up. It allowed me to think and plan for further training. I never believed that graduation meant an end to study and learning. I approached my calling with renewed energy and the resolve to continue to improve my ability to serve.

At the time of graduation, the ceremony can for a moment seem like the severing of one's ties. This was only a momentary break for me. I was a mature person now, managing for myself, responsible for my own deeds and wishes, planning my own future, moving forward and looking for additional challenges.

And I did all that.

The graduation services were held on September 26,

1940 in the Nurse's Home Conference Room at Brewster. Eight of the nurses who had entered in 1937 were there to claim their diplomas.

Our speaker, the Rev. Albert J. Kisssling, pastor of the Riverside Presbyterian Church, urged us to "move forward and find our places in the world of professional nursing." He stressed the importance of our dedication and our ability to serve.

Dr. and Mrs. W. R. Schnauss were present for the event. Dr. Schnauss was medical director, and Mrs. Schnauss had made regular visits to the school throughout the year. They represented the Women's Home Missionary Society of the Methodist Episcopal Church, headquartered in Minneapolis, Minnesota. Their visits and concern were important to the hospital staff, training school and the management of the total operation. Other concerns had been safety and, of course, the best care of the patients that could be rendered.

Proper nursing methods and procedures in clinical areas, as well as our individual academic successes, were always an important part of our ability to serve.

My first job as a nurse at Brewster was in the Crippled Children's Ward. I replaced another classmate, Irene Parrish. The Crippled Children's Department was under the medical supervision of State of Florida physicians, Drs. Lovejoy, Ford and Martin.

The duties in the ward were demanding and physically exhausting at times. But I learned a lot about leadership, supervision, child care, physician's orders, and working with the Public Health nurses in the follow-up programs.

Shortly after my assignment to the children's ward the newly-hired superintendent, Miss Florence Jones, R. N., called together the members of the graduating class who were still at Brewster. She gave us application papers for membership in the American Red Cross Nursing Service.

Prior to 1941 the Red Cross had not accepted applications from Brewster nurses. But Brewster, having met all the requirements, was accredited and perhaps the hospital's administrative staff failed to press for the opening for lack of interest until Miss Jones came to the school.

Miss Jones, who went on to become one of Brewster's outstanding directors, was a white administrator sent to the school from Hampton University, a colored school in Hampton, Virginia. At Brewster there were colored physicians, colored interns, colored residents, colored head nurses and colored clerical and lab employees.

Miss Jones, sensitive to the needs of colored nurses, worked hard to improve race relations at all levels of the nursing profession. Her efforts helped improve the total operation of Brewster Hospital and its nursing school while opening new opportunities for colored nurses.

Now the timing was right what with a world war looming and changing racial attitudes towards colored nurses by local, state and national nurses organizations.

At first, few of us paid much attention to Miss Jones' invitation. But some days later I sat down and carefully looked through the papers, and approached the chief medical doctor, Dr. I. E. Williams.

Dr. Williams was an outstanding physician. He strongly believed in progress, efficiency and self-improvement.

He urged me to follow Miss Jones' advice, and he was quite pleased that the American Red Cross had taken an interest in recruiting Brewster nurses. He also offered to assist me.

On his sterling recommendation, I filled out the forms and submitted them to the American Red Cross. It would be several weeks before I could learn whether or not I would be permitted membership in the Red Cross.

During the weeks of late 1940 we heard much about the fighting in Europe. There were rumors of war heard from every radio. I didn't realize what hints of my future the radio news was bringing, that I soon would become involved as a nurse in the largest world war — "The Big One." We just kept hearing the terrible news for weeks and months.

At about this time, our hospital was visited by the Executive Secretary of the National Association of Colored Graduate Nurses, an organization which served to support the advancement of colored nurses.

Mrs. Mabel K. Staupers, was the association's first executive director, and president when the group was dissolved in 1951.

Her purpose, and that of her association, was to promote equality among nurses and to support the effort to enroll nurses in local nurses' associations and in the American Red Cross Nursing Service. Once so enrolled, nurses from Brewster also would qualify for assignment in the Army Nurse Corps as commissioned Army officers.

Unaware of Mrs. Staupers' timely visit and noble purpose, my fellow nurses and I took little notice of her presence at Brewster. But thanks to her prominence in the National Nurses Association, and her channels of communication throughout the nation, she was able to bring about many important social and professional changes for colored nurses.

Several weeks had passed since I mailed the application for membership to the American Red Cross Nursing Service. Not many of us gave much thought to the possible acceptance of colored nurses from Brewster by the Red Cross. We hadn't known that Mrs. Staupers and others were working so strenuously to establish our eligibility in that organization.

Little did we know that this was to be the beginning of a new era for colored nurses across the United States and for the Brewster School of Nursing's ability to qualify also.

It was the most fervent desire of Miss Jones and other concerned members of the hospital staff that the hospital eventually would be accepted. Their purpose was twofold: establishing membership in the Red Cross service was in itself an important professional standing; and Brewster graduates would also win eligibility to be U. S. Army nurses.

One day several weeks later I received an urgent call from the superintendent's office requesting my immediate presence. She told me I had received a letter of acceptance from the Red Cross, and she wanted me to know about it right away! She was so pleased to receive the good news at last that Brewster School of Nursing was now a member of the Red Cross Service.

I read the letter, excited and delighted to see that I was accepted and now would appear on the national roster, eligible for call as a nurse in case of disaster, and also eligible for military service.

Miss Jones was eager to inform the staff and board members that the school had been accepted, and it was through my effort, *by filling out the form*, that the first Brewster graduate had received full membership.

With membership now granted to me, I became more concerned about the war and the fighting. The media continued to report ominous news. We Americans were becoming more war-minded every day. The need for nurses to care for the troops stationed near the war zone was heard over the airwaves.

At the time I was assigned as a staff nurse in the outpatient clinic at Brewster. The clinic was held five days a week and was well attended. All major services were available to the people in the neighborhood of the hospital. The clinic was well staffed and organized.

Patients needing surgical service were seen by Drs. Duncan and Daniels. Others in need of medical service saw Dr. Williams, the chief of medical services.

Drs. Ward and Campbell saw to obstetrics, Drs. Brown and Thomas cared for eye, nose and throat patients, and Drs. Ford, Lovejoy and Martin cared for children under the Florida Crippled Children Service.

One of the largest and best attended of the clinical departments was the one under Dr. Schell, Sr. and his staff, treating venereal diseases. After hours and during emergencies, the house physicians cared for patients. Care was always available.

My duty assignment at the clinic was interesting as well as beneficial, for not only were the hours easier to work, but I had the opportunity to instruct and evaluate the follow-up care. This chance to learn by taking on more responsibility had been another important advantage of the Brewster School of Nursing and remained so during my employment at the Hospital.

I was grateful for the chance to continue working at Brewster following graduation, but I knew the normal tour of duty and pay scale offered at Brewster would not entice one to stay indefinitely.

I felt good, as well as loyal to my alma mater, but I also felt an urge to advance professionally. I consulted with several local public health nurses and took a week off duty to travel home to Atlanta. Once home, I discussed the opportunities in public health nursing with my older sister, Mamie Catherine Ivory, who was a public health nurse in the health department of Dekalb County, near Atlanta.

She and all the nurses who had vast experience in public health urged me to follow my dream. Public health nursing had always required the very best nurses, willing to travel, and with leadership and teaching abilities. It still requires all that.

To be a productive nurse, one must be well-trained in all aspects of nursing care, and be able to teach and demonstrate health care, and to have a true love for people regardless of their race, creed or color. A public health nurse must have a deeply spiritual love of mankind. With these and other requirements in mind, I was advised by my sister Catherine to think seriously about my interest. Catherine suggested that if I continued to feel the same way about public health nursing, I should attend an approved public health nursing school.

In 1941 in my area there were two approved basic public health nursing schools, each offering one-year courses. One school, Peabody in Tennessee, was for white nurses. The other, Hampton Institute in Hampton, Virginia, was where I applied immediately.

I was making plans to enroll under the program in Virginia when I received news from the United States Army Nurse Corps.

At Grady Hospital in Atlanta during affiliate year (above). Brewster celebrates its first Red Cross nurse, April, 1941.

Visiting Mama and the family on first leave from Ft. Bragg, March, 1942.

First group of colored nurses commissioned by the U. S. Army Nurse Corps, Ft. Bragg, NC, 1941.

Among the first brand new Second Lieutenants were (left to right) nurses Della Ramey, Louise Jacobs, Gertrude M. Ivory and Rose Johnson, with newspapermen in May, 1941.
The first group of colored U. S. Army nurses saw service in Monrovia, Liberia, West Africa during 1943 and 1944.

CHAPTER SEVEN

United States Army Nurse Corps

The war was spreading. The news was not good. It seemed America would soon be part of it.

Much was required and expected of those who were available, and by joining the American Red Cross Service I had made myself available.

Well, it happened. Only a short time after my acceptance into the Red Cross Service, I received a letter from the War Department stating that I was one of the first fifty-six colored nurses in the United States to qualify for a commission in the Army Nurse Corps. The letter also contained information about readiness for military service.

This first correspondence as to my part in the conflict

was dated April 23, 1941 and came from the Fourth Corps Area of the War Department, located in Atlanta.

Signed by chief nurse Captain Mary Gavin, her letter stated that I had been referred to her command area from the American Red Cross roster as being ready for commission in the Army Nurse Corps. I was expected to be on active duty on or about May 1, 1941, according to the letter.

It seemed that my name was showing up on various rosters. I didn't know it, but there were a lot of people working on my behalf, all of them intent on sending me off to war.

There were only two areas at the time where colored nurses were assigned for duty: Fort Bragg, North Carolina, and Camp Livingston, Louisiana.

Capt. Gavin allowed me to make the choice. I talked to people I knew, and they all advised that I choose the North Carolina post because that state was far more advanced, in matters of race relations, than Louisiana.

At that time, there were three criteria that could keep me out of the military. If I were the mother of a minor child, or practicing midwifery, or instructing in a nursing school, I would not have to go. None of those applied to me.

So I was off to war.

Miss Jones, superintendent at Brewster Hospital, was extremely pleased, too.

In our correspondence Capt. Gavin was very kind and understanding, and made it easy for me to accept such a large challenge. She seemed to know I was frightened, but also that I wanted the opportunity to serve in the Army. She knew I had the right spirit and dedication.

In the weeks that followed plans were completed for my military assignment. I made my decision known to Capt. Gavin. She seemed pleased when I told her I would accept the job and go to Fort Bragg.

My friends at Brewster were also pleased, if not tickled. My school was experiencing another first: the first of its graduates to go into the Army Nurse Corps, among the first of colored nurses anywhere who were doing that.

There was a round of interviews with the news media, patriotic teas, farewell gifts and good wishes from the staff and friends.

I was commissioned into the United States Army Nurse Corps on April 25, 1941 as a Second Lieutenant. Travel orders required me to report to Fort Bragg, North Carolina. I was to go by first class Pullman service from Jacksonville, via Atlanta. That was particularly exciting to me since I had never traveled via first class before, and I looked forward to the experience.

According to the orders, I was to make my own reservations, and was advised to call the railroad myself, for travel on April 30, 1941. That would put me at Fort Bragg on May 1, ready to report for active duty.

I made the reservations by phone and every thing seemed all right. But when I got to the station, still in civilian clothes, all hell broke loose. I had not told the ticket agent I was colored, and in the Deep South in that era, colored people almost never traveled first class. The train was delayed while the conductor and other trainmen decided what to do. Finally I was directed to a Pullman car porter who, I immediately realized, did not like the disruption.

"Girl," he said to me, "you are out of your place, thinking you can ride in the Pullman area!"

His attitude surprised me. I thought he would have been proud of me, going into the Army Nurse Corps. But, no. To him I was just more work and trouble.

I felt badly about the scene, but it could not have been avoided.

I was traveling on orders from the United State Army Nurse Corps. Nevertheless, it was the first real racial discrimination I had encountered from another colored person.

For a few moments all the wonderful things that had happened to me, and all the admiration I had received from the staff at Brewster School of Nursing, and all the effort and support they had expended in my training, blew up in the reality of racial prejudice.

Fortunately, it didn't stop me.

It didn't take long for the impact to pass and for me to begin fighting back. I quickly snapped out of my mental daze, dismissed my hesitation and doubts about why I was there, and came alive.

I walked over to that porter and looked him straight in the eye, and then I let him have it.

Then and there, I demanded the first class traveling accommodations to which I was entitled, and I reminded him that I was traveling under government orders as a recently commissioned officer in the Army Nurse Corps. Furthermore, I told him, I was a force to be reckoned with.

For a short moment I thought I had won him over to my corner, but I was wrong. He didn't frighten easily. He was probably a long-time employee of the railroad, with years of experience that had taught him well what his responsibilities were.

Without batting an eye, he replied, "Girl, again I tell you that you got to be put in your place and I am the one to do it!"

With this, I decided I had better cooperate, whatever his plan was.

He marched me off to the rear of the train, mumbling all the way. I followed, hoping this would end the conflict. After all, I had been reared to have respect for older persons, and especially older colored men.

When we got to the rear of the train, to my surprise I discovered that the porter had arranged for me to have a private drawing room, all to myself.

It was a beautiful sleeping car, with all the amenities I would require. I was thrilled and amazed. He was relieved and happy, too, to have his problem at an end.

"I put this buzzer here," he said. "Don't leave this room. I don't want you mixing with my people. If you need anything, you ring the buzzer." He had even placed a portable toilet in the stateroom.

Well, I soon learned that I am one who does not sleep well on a moving train. I rang that buzzer fairly constantly through the night, and I'm sure that man was more than glad early the next morning in Florence, South Carolina, to see me off his train and onto a troop train. But he did have some parting words, which I think he gave me in a

81

kindly way.

"I am pleased to see that you are going into the service," he said, "but you had better settle down or you will start another war about this traveling business. You young upstarts want to change everything overnight. It can't be done. Be patient and everything will improve."

I remembered the old gentleman's philosophy. It was well taken. He had weathered racial problems all through the years and he knew well that conditions would improve some day, maybe not for him and his fellow porters, but for the younger generations to come.

He knew, and I understood, that he was forced to follow the customs of the day. He was older and had been on the job too long to cause trouble. I think that was the only reason he was impatient with me.

As I left the train to transfer to the troop train bound for Fort Bragg, even after our disagreement, I felt a kinship with him. I thanked him and wished him good health and happiness.

Arriving several hours later at the medical area of Fort Bragg, I was immediately escorted to Nursing Headquarters of Station Hospital Number 2 for processing. I was fingerprinted, given ANC Serial #N-726319, and isued regulation uniforms including capes, shoes, and insignia.

Then I was assigned to Nurses Barracks Number 21.

The next four to six weeks were busy with Army orientation. One policy of the Army that struck me was the rule against fraternization with enlisted personnel.

I was told that I was one of only fifty-six colored nurses selected to fill the initial quota for the nursing branch of the service. Later the quota was lifted due to the need for additional nurses. Army nursing was very different from civilian nursing. The hospital buildings were crude barracks and the hours were longer, although the pay was good.

A typical day on duty was a 12-hour shift, usually in charge of an open ward of twenty-six beds. The buildings were temporary with open screened sides, long corridors and large porches where some patients could go to smoke and play cards. They could be cold and scarey at night as we made the rounds by flashlight.

Our first the assignments were for routine nursing work but by late 1942 and early 1943 we saw a small change. Some colored nurses were named ward managers and supervised colored and white nurses. There were few real problems that could not be worked out; most nurses knew why they were there and went about providing good care for the men.

It was soon apparent that, in addition to regular nursing duties, the nurse was the one who provided hope, faith and loving care for these young men away from home – she was the mother, sister or wife who was far away.

You had to keep reminding yourself not to become too attached to the patients.

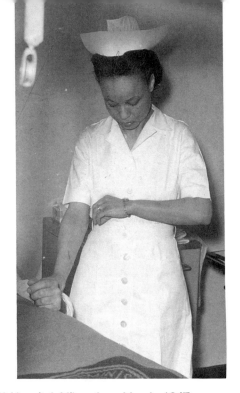

Nurse Bertram on duty at VA Hospital, Milwaukee, March, 1947
(above) and with colleagues in Central Supply (below).

CHAPTER EIGHT

Military And Foreign Duty

My first tour of duty at Fort Bragg was from May 1, 1941 to February 8, 1943.

Fort Bragg was a very large Army station with permanent and temporary (station) hospitals. I was assigned to Station Hospital Number 2, where all the colored doctors and nurses were assigned.

Among our group of colored nurses, all commissioned from the Red Cross roster, were Della Ramey from North Carolina, Rosa Johnson from Grady Hospital in Atlanta, and Emily Perkins, Ruth Briggs and Louise Jacobs from Lincoln School of Nursing in New York.

The nurses' barracks were Number 21, and colored doctors were housed in Barracks 22. The buildings were temporary, the streets were unpaved, and there were muddy walkways everywhere.

This was quite a change from the beautiful hospital

grounds at Brewster and the city of Jacksonville, Florida. But I realized I was going to have to accept the change of scenery and learn to relax in an Army environment. It was not really very difficult.

The first thing I did after unpacking was to write letters, one to my mother and the second to Miss Jones. I knew she would want to know the details of my trip and how I survived from the moment I boarded the train until I registered at the station hospital.

I didn't miss a single detail. Miss Jones had been so helpful and supportive in my various adventures, encouraging me when problems arose, always making it easier to overcome and understand and accept difficulties and new challenges.

Miss Jones was proud that Brewster School of Nursing was among the first hospitals responsible for training colored nurses, and to qualify in the first U. S. Army quota of fifty-six colored nurses to be commissioned. Until her retirement, she continued to work in maintaining the standards and reputation of my school. This time it was one of her graduates being among the first colored nurses to report for active duty at Fort Bragg.

All through my tour of duty stateside, as well as on foreign assignment, we stayed in touch. She sent small personal gifts and words of encouragement, always reporting on the school and keeping it foremost in both our minds.

After the rush of admission to the hospital area was completed, I was able to settle down and relax. I was really grateful for the privilege of being part of such a huge medical complex and working with so many wonderful people.

It was a moment of maturing for me, too, for I had to think that all this medical talent was being assembled because of the coming war that would change all our lives.

I met many wonderful and interesting people among the nurses, doctors, patients and paramedics. These people enriched my life and provided memories that would last forever. Among them was Esther Steward-Mc-Larin of Springfield, Massachusetts, a nurse who is my best friend to this day.

Another was Irma Carole, a white WAC (Women's Army Corps) from Iowa who had never been exposed to colored people.

We met when she was assigned to my ward, #85 Orthopedic, and would touch my hand or arm just to see if my color would rub off. She was sweet and kind and we became the best of friends, staying in touch long after the war was over.

In the next two years we developed into a large medical family. We were from all parts of the United States, with various backgrounds, but mostly with the same purpose and philosophy: to serve our country and give the best medical care we were capable of providing.

The Army hospital routines were different from civilian hospitals. Many adjustments were necessary, but the purpose of care to the sick and injured was the same.

The colored nurses in Barracks 21 had to learn to make life worth living. We had about twenty-four nurses to a barracks and each was provided with a private sleeping room with maid service. There was a large day room equipped with record players, radios, games and books. Some of the nurses were bridge players and others played whist or pinochle. Some of us went to town for socializing, too.

There were social and intellectual activities, too. While a group might sew or knit, some interesting topic would be discussed by a selected person. Subjects included current events, medical findings, religion and books. Even the social graces, dining out and modeling came in for discussion. Sports included volleyball and tennis.

The time we spent with each other was also helpful in supporting those who were having problems in adjusting to the military style of living. We were like a group of sisters.

When convenient, some nurses attended religious services on the post with the enlisted men of the 76th and 77th Field Artillery. They also attended services in the churches of the little town of Fayetteville, North Carolina. Most of the services on the post, and many social events were held in the open air.

During World War II commissioned officers were not permitted to socialize with enlisted men. Nurses were not permitted to be married, either. If they married, they were removed from duty.

The colored doctors' quarters were located in the area. Most of the doctors were married and went home on weekends, or their families came to visit them on the post. Visiting with these families helped the nurses tremendously. Contact and communication with them kept us all in touch with civilian life.

In the fall of 1941 the Army built a beautiful club for colored officers across from our area. This helped also, because the club provided an opportunity for social activities for Army personnel as well as our guests from town when they came to visit.

Since segregation was the pattern of the races then, we had our own dining room. The dining room, like the officers' club, was fully staffed at all times. Our dining room also was open to visitors. When they accompanied us we could take them to meals for a nominal fee.

I was easily able to make the transition to Army life because of the excellent training I had gotten at Brewster. I felt the support of the staff, and Miss Jones, and the enthusiasm they encouraged in their students, was a valuable carryover into my military career and later assignments.

At Fort Bragg we kept busy with our assigned duties. We also listened to the radio for news of the developing warfare. And finally, in the fall of 1942, we learned that our 25th Station Hospital was to be sent overseas.

We were to go to West Africa. On February 8, 1943, a group of colored nurses left Fort Bragg by troop train bound for Camp Kilmer, New Jersey, where we joined a contingent of other nurses. In all, we numbered thirty colored nurses under the command of First Lieutenant Susan Freeman, a colored nursing supervisor from Freedmon Hospital in Washington, D. C.

After several days at Camp Kilmer we reported to Staten Island, New York, where the *James Parker*, a huge troopship, was ready for sailing. Next stop was the beautiful city of Casablanca in French West Africa. On

March 10, 1943 we embarked for our final destination, Monrovia, Liberia, West Africa.

Immediately upon arriving we learned that there were certain health problems in Africa, chief among them malaria and the lack of proper sanitary drinking water. We were required to take all the known anti-malarial medications, a rule as important as our 24-hour dress code.

However, despite the best precautions, rigidly enforced, all of the nurses, myself included, at one time or another suffered malaria. Sometimes the attacks of the fever were mild, other times acute. Some of us experienced complications and many continued to suffer attacks three to five years after discharge from the service.

But something good did come of my malaria illness. One day, while feeling better after an attack of the fever and chills, I noticed a non-commissioned officer visiting the hospital ward where I was being treated. I asked who he was. He told me he was Staff Sergeant Robert Bruce Bertram, attached to the 25th Station Hospital as a member of the clerical staff.

There was immediate chemistry between us. I noticed that Robert was young, handsome, quiet, soft-spoken and articulate.

I liked what I saw about Robert and knew I had to find a way to tell him I wanted to know him better. I wrote him a short note and gave a native boy a chocolate bar to deliver it. I didn't know how Robert would respond, but to my pleasant surprise he answered immediately.

Later, after my discharge from the malaria ward, we

met formally and decided we felt the same about each other. After a few dates, Robert asked me to marry him after we returned to the United States.

Of course, I readily accepted and began planning the event, which eventually came about two years later. We were married on November 20, 1945 in Louisville, Kentucky. Our union is now in its forty-fifth year and still strong.

Meanwhile, we had a war to win.

After serving nine months on foreign soil, the entire thirty-nurse contingent returned to the United States for further medical treatment of complications from malaria. We were sent to Camp Livingston, Louisiana, arriving on December 6, 1943.

Following treatment, some of the nurses were cleared for reassignment to duty in the States as well as overseas. But I continued to have recurrences of malaria, fever, weakness and general malaise. In fact, I felt that living in Louisiana was about as unhealthy as living in West Africa. The mosquitoes were as active and just as big.

I continued to feel bad. I was given permission to request a transfer out of Camp Livingston and return to Fort Bragg for health reasons.

The request was granted and several weeks later, on March 30, 1944 I was on my way back to Hospital Number 2, Barracks 21, Fort Bragg, to serve the remaining tour of Army duty.

Nine of the nurses who served in the West African area of the European-Middle East Theater received letters of commendation from the U. S. Surgeon General for service beyond the call of duty. I was proud to be one of them.

Arriving back at Fort Bragg for a second tour of duty was just like coming home. I was happy to be back.

Shortly after my reassignment to Fort Bragg, in the summer of 1944, I was placed on the medical wards to work with a team which was studying the use of two new drugs, penicillin and streptomycin.

The study was confined to the patients of the two wards, and there were several special things the team wanted to know about side effects, if any were observed.

This was the first controlled use of penicillin.

The penicillin was in an oil mixture. Nurses were instructed to carry the bottle in their uniform pockets so as to have the medicine at body temperature when it was administered. It could not be chilled or warmed.

The mixture was difficult to withdraw because of the oil component. If it was too warm the penicillin would seep out.

All of a patient's fluids were collected and refrigerated. The urine was placed in sterile flasks. Stools were saved and analyzed by the lab staff. Blood was drawn from a vein every four hours and refrigerated. All external and internal symptoms were monitored and recorded. Incorrect speech, such as slurring, as well as elevated temperature, headache, diarrhea, vomiting, redness and itching were identified, recorded and filed for the medical team.

A physician was always available for advice on the necessary treatment of the patient.

The team was very large but worked well together. It was a pleasant assignment and a rewarding experience because of the close study I was able to make of the two drugs. I saw them come into more common use in our hospital and in other medical facilities.

There was, in fact, a revolution in drug therapy because of both drugs, and I am proud to have been part of the original studies that contributed to the widespread use of these life-saving medicines — penicillin and streptomycin. They, and other anti-biotics, came to be called miracle drugs and were widely used in the post-war era.

I was told that this type of observation was also carried on at other hospital areas. There were other wonder drugs studied and later released for administration to the sick and suffering soon after the war was over, drugs that have contributed greatly to faster recoveries and prolonging life.

This assignment in the medical wards was one of the high moments in patient care that I enjoyed while in the Army. The commitment, the high quality of nursing procedures, and the professional excellence required of each participant made the study outstanding and of lasting importance.

One other assignment, the final one of my Army career, was to give care to forty-six young, white wounded soldiers who had been severely injured during the Normandy beachhead landing on June 6, 1944. This assignment was one of the more moving services I had the privilege of rendering during my entire tour of duty.

The men, all on stretchers, were coming in on three hospital airplanes. These soldiers were enroute to various Army general hospitals throughout the country. All were paraplegics, paralyzed from the waist down. This was to be a short stop-over for them.

The chief nurse ordered me to open a closed hospital ward for them and to set up the ward with all necessary personnel and supplies to provide the men with the best nursing care possible.

She emphasized that nothing was to be left undone for these men. No vital services were too large, no creature comfort too small for them.

The flight nurses were to bring them to us from the incoming planes. The nurse who was assigned to assist me with their care came down the ramp, looked into the ward, turned and went back. She did not enter the ward or report her reason for not doing so to the chief nurse.

I was very busy, but not too busy to notice; I did feel that her behavior was racially inspired. She was white and I was colored, and she would have been under my direction. So it was easier for her not to enter. I assume this, anyway.

I had no time to stop and talk with her. I had patients in my care and no time to lose. These men were my responsibility and I intended to give them the best possible care.

Several corpsmen were sent in to assist me as well. They were well-trained and capable of giving good care. They, too, were veterans of combat duty.

All the patients were given complete baths, their bodies oiled and their hair shampooed. We changed dressings and paid special attention to prosthetic limbs and other support systems.

After we had taken care of their medical needs, we began to see to other things we could do for them. We called in the barbers, and the Red Cross Grey Ladies brought them fresh flowers, fruit, telephone and telegraph service, making it possible for the men to call home and talk with their families and girl friends.

This was a tremendous boost for the men. They were happy later when it was time to eat. A well-balanced meal was served, everyone's spirit was good, and they appeared comfortable and ready to complete their transfer to a general hospital nearer their home.

In late afternoon the Army flight nurses returned for their patients. They seemed pleased and happy when they observed the patients' appearance and their state of readiness for further travel.

On leaving the hospital ward, the entire group expressed thanks and gratitude for the care they had received. The chief nurse and the medical director of Station Hospital Number 2 also came on the ward and expressed their satisfaction over the care of the patients.

In a short time we would see our forty-six paraplegic soldiers airborne again, enroute to comfortable hospital beds where they would receive the best medical and surgical care available to American wounded.

In all the nursing assignments and experiences I encountered on duty, either stateside or in foreign assignments, nothing provided me more pleasure and more humility than caring for those forty-six men. Caring for them made me think about their futures. They were young men who would have preferred to return home to their families and their communities walking like others. But they were victims of war and destruction. They were not to be forgotten.

Reunion in 1987, fifty years after starting nurse training at Brewster.

Brig. Gen. Hazel Johnson and Mrs. Bertram help mark the 80thanniversary of the U. S. Army Nurse Corps, Walter Reed Hospital, Washington, D. C.

CHAPTER NINE

Back To Civilian Life

It was October, 1945, and the fighting was over. Soldiers, officers and medical units were returning to America. And in spite of all our travels, there was no place like home, no doubt about it.

We who had experienced overseas assignments were also experiencing less action stateside. It gave us a feeling of relief throughout the Army posts across the land. There was much to be happy about. The war was over.

Regular commissions in the Army Nurse Corps were being offered to members of the nursing staff and some temporarily-commissioned nurses would remain in the service. I recall being asked to remain on active duty. Much as I had enjoyed serving in the Army Nurse Corps, and despite my dedication to the soldiers, I had made a commitment to marry my Army sweetheart. It wasn't easy, but I had to turn the Army down.

I had a date with a splendid young man and I couldn't keep him waiting.

Nurses were summoned to the headquarters of the medical command and thanked for their service. Citations, status and Army ratings were reviewed and a 201 file presented along with travel expenses. Those of us who were leaving were joyful but we all left a bit of ourselves at the center.

I was discharged as a First Lieutenant chief nurse after four years, nine months and thirteen days of active duty. I had seventy-two days of accumulated annual leave and sick leave, for which I was compensated, and detailed to a troop train at High Point, North Carolina. With separation papers and train ticket, I boarded the Southern Express on October 10, 1945 and headed for Atlanta and home.

I had a date to keep with Staff Sergeant Robert Bertram, the young man I had met and fallen in love with in Africa. I had promised to marry him when the war was over, and after my return to Atlanta I began making those plans.

Robert was a graduate of Lincoln Institute, Louisville, Kentucky's separate but equal high school for colored students. He was in his second year of study at the Kentucky State College in Frankfort when he was inducted into the Army. Later, when the 25th Station Hospital was activated he was one of the men selected for training for medical services on foreign soil.

When Robert and I met in Monrovia, and discovered our feelings for each other, we were both aware of the

military's policy forbidding fraternization between commissioned officers and enlisted personnel. We had
decided to play it cool until discharge from the service.
During our short and limited courtship in Liberia, our
only communication was through an African man known
as "small boy" who did not speak or read English. Robert
and I would exchange notes and have them delivered by
this man; the "postal" fee usually was a bar of chocolate
candy.

We were married November 20, 1945 in Louisville,
Kentucky. It was another event I will not forget.

Because of the limited time we both had for the
marriage formalities, we rushed through it. The Justice
of the Peace, who knew my husband-to-be and was from
his home area in Wayne County, Kentucky, married us.
His being a friend helped a lot.

We had hired a broken-down taxi in Lexington to
drive us to Louisville. The driver waited for us and only
charged $30, including the return trip to Lexington.

Robert caught a plane out at about 4 p.m. and
returned to duty with the 732nd Sanitary Environment
Company in Charleston, South Carolina.

It was a quick wedding ceremony but it has been a
long and happy marriage. Many quick marriages such as
ours don't last long, but in spite of the rushed plans, our
has worked out extremely well.

Following our marriage, we moved to Milwaukee,
Wisconsin, where we both attended graduate school
under the GI Bill. I enrolled in Marquette University's

Public Health studies program. Robert attended engineering school. Earlier, following his discharge from the Army, he had completed his schooling in Kentucky, receiving training as an electrocardiagram and electroencephalogram medical technician.

I recall, when I attempted to enroll in the Public Health School, as always, the indications of prejudice were there, directed against those individuals who attempted to seek self-improvement. I encountered some resentment and was often reminded that only one colored nurse would be in the class. I guess they felt this would cause me to change my mind, and not enroll. It was too bad that they were not aware of my strong intent to study.

I remember some staff members who told me about one colored student who had attended Marquette University before me. He had been the only colored student in his class and he had excelled in all areas, especially sports. He was Ralph Metcalf, the outstanding track star, and now a large photograph of him hung on the wall in the main building of the school.

Somehow, each time I walked past his picture I was reminded that I, too, must excel in my studies. I secretly promised myself, and Metcalf, that I would study hard and would not leave any unfavorable feelings in the university's School of Public Health.

But as a race-conscious person, I was surely proud of his record. Still, I was there to study nursing on my own merits, and when I left Marquette I left some favorable memories of my own.

When Robert enrolled, his experience was just the

opposite. The staff he encountered was cordial, helpful, friendly and supportive.

We finally finished our studies and secured good employment with the City of Milwaukee. Robert took a job as a stationary engineer with the Milwaukee Coke & Gas Co. I began work as a public health nurse.

This was a fantastic opportunity, as Milwaukee had the best medical and social services of most cities, and certainly the best all-around community services in the Midwest. The caseload in my district was composed of people of many ethnic backgrounds. During the time I was working as a public health nurse there, my patients were mostly Jewish or German immigrants, and a small number of American Negroes. There were small numbers of Swedish, Norwegian and Indian populations, as well as some Polish and Italian people, too.

Regardless of their national origins, the immigrants spoke a mixture of languages. This created a problem for me, because at first it was difficult for me to communicate with them. But as always, when confronted with a problem, I readily accepted the challenge and promptly found ways to overcome it.

My first choice to solve this problem was through the younger generations of the families. The children had social relationships with other children, both foreign-born and native-born. These younger Americans had generally learned to master English as well as their native tongue, and this was to the advantage of the patients and me because it made direct communication possible. Through the children, I was able to understand the needs of my patients and serve them.

I learned early that an effective health worker had to be patient, a good listener, imaginative, flexible and full of compassion. By working with ethnic groups I learned to recognize and speak a few foreign words. With that, some sign language, and the children, we always managed to get along.

My district was truly a melting pot, and I had no problems with the people in it. Many medical and social problems existed, but with cooperation and help from the Public Health Service, the people were healthy in the main.

One outstanding thing I remember most was giving instructions and demonstrations in food exchanges to foreign families. Two common dishes were rice and broccoli. Every ethnic group often served both, so I had to learn many different ways to prepare these foods. Every group had its own customs for doing them, using various seasonings and methods of preparation. I learned them all from my patients, and it made me a better cook.

I really learned from one Jewish family, not only about cooking, but about the Old Testament as well. In public service we were not expected to discuss religion, but I could listen and I did enjoy their comments.

I worked closely with other agencies in the community in bringing good health and social adjustment to family life among these new and old Americans.

Likewise, I also learned from the German ladies how to cook. They were excellent cooks, and I found their foods delightful, especially their home-made breads, jams, and wine. And their rhubarb and strawberry cream pies were a delight.

In contrast to the strong patient-nurse relationships I had in so many homes, I am sorry to say that I did encounter problems with the nursing administration, especially the Department of Certification. After working for more than six months with the Milwaukee Visiting Nurses Association, I learned that the Wisconsin State Nurses Association questioned my credentials as to the state requirements for certification.

The problem was not subject matter, but the relatively small average daily bed capacity at Brewster.

This really concerned me because this was the first time my nursing background had ever been questioned. Always before as far as theory and practice were concerned, my training had been acceptable in other states. I immediately sought to correct the problem.

I contacted Brewster at once for assistance and direction. I learned that Wisconsin had established laws long before I arrived dealing not only with the theory of nursing arts, but setting a high daily bed capacity requirement as a criterion for full nurse reciprocity with other states.

Brewster Hospital, with only a fifty-bed daily capacity, was not acceptable under Wisconsin nursing requirements. I was informed I would have to ask the Wisconsin State Board of Nursing to take their exams. Meanwhile, I would have to discontinue my teaching (planned parenthood courses) and home health care.

I applied and was given permission to take the boards, and ten years after I had taken my original nursing board exams in Florida, I passed Wisconsin's, and returned to my teaching and demonstration classes.

I went even further, and took the Master Public Health Nurse test, known then as the National League of Nursing Test. I passed it, and this made me eligible to work as a public health nurse in any state.

It seemed there was always some interruption such as this preventing steady work progress for me. Although it is not unusual for many people to be confronted by problems of one kind or another, causing frustration and even failure, I felt I didn't deserve that kind of pressure. So I simply became determined to surmount such obstacles.

With this new attitude I determined to move ahead, trying to avoid unpleasantness while maintaining my determination. When you feel you deserve to improve, and you can find ways to do it, you must not hesitate to bring about changes even if that incurs someone else's dislike. Your own self-esteem is the proper goal; you must be true to yourself.

Returning to the classroom and to the district as a home health care field teacher, I worked successfully for eight years for the City of Milwaukee. Other than the administrative problem just mentioned above, it was fun working there as a public health nurse.

In winter, the days were long and cold, with a lot of snow making it difficult to get around, but I thoroughly enjoyed the work. In spring and summer, it was delightful working outside. On a clear day you could smell the odors of the local breweries mixing with the delicious smell of freshly baked bread.

Milwaukee has beautiful, wide, clean streets, each then lined with large, old elm trees whose branches touched high above the pavement, dappling the sidewalks with spots of sunlight to warm anyone walking there.

During those eight years, I took time out for one year to give birth to a beautiful baby girl. Rita Kathleen was born on April 30, 1950.

Becoming a mother, I thought, would slow me down and perhaps even dampen some of the light, free spirit with which I am blessed. But becoming a mother was no match for anything I had experienced previously. I enjoyed motherhood and felt then, and I still feel, that becoming a mother is the grandest and most noble feeling a woman can have.

No career accomplishment compares with it. I was grateful for every minute I could spend caring for my baby.

On our first visit to the well-baby clinic after Rita's birth, I was informed that she had been born with a congenital birth defect known as Patent Ductus Arteriosis (PDA), and would require close supervision for the first five years of her life.

The prognosis was unfavorable, and there was doubt that she would ever enjoy the full life that comes to most people: attending school, going to college, getting married and having children.

All of my physical and mental energies were turned toward giving her the best possible care. She responded well to therapy and eventually overcame the odds against her.

Rita accomplished her goals, graduating from Central State University in Xenia, Ohio, enjoying a successful marriage and giving birth to a normal baby girl on July 12, 1981. They named her Amber Maria.

Through all of the trying times together, the efforts, adjustments, sacrifices and caring, this really was an accomplishment for my daughter because she beat the odds. But the family, of course, did have to make some adjustments.

Because of the extreme cold and the long winters in Wisconsin, we had to leave Milwaukee for a warmer climate. In the fall of 1955 the family moved to Dayton, Ohio where the winters were less severe and somewhat shorter than in Wisconsin.

It was during this time that Rita's general health began to show rapid improvement. The Patent Ductus closed, resulting in an improvement in growth and development. At age six, we were able to enroll her in public school, although there was always a need for close observation and support to maintain her health.

CHAPTER TEN

Dayton, Ohio

Shortly after arriving in Dayton I went to work as a public health nurse for the City of Dayton. Robert joined the medical technician staff of the Veterans Medical Center in Dayton, where he worked for the next thirty years.

I was assigned to the lower east end of town. The area, a district known as Number 10, was populated mostly by southern whites who had migrated from Appalachia to Dayton in the hope of finding factory jobs.

There was no language barrier here because almost all of my clients were of American backgrounds, with just a few of German descent. I encountered no real racial problems, except that some of the older men did not feel comfortable around me. But they might have felt that way about any woman health-care provider.

At any rate, there was ample need for health care, meal planning, well-child care, pre-school care, proper housing, medical care and general welfare.

It was a busy district. There were always challenging

projects for improving the health and welfare of people struggling to adapt to the stressful cultural and financial changes in their own lives. The churches and merchants were helpful as were such other agencies as the Family and Children's Services General Relief.

The community's physicians, ministers and schools in time became my chief allies, and they would respond to virtually every request I made of them.

During the late 1950s and early 1960s there was new emphasis toward providing mental health services. For years much time, money and effort had been focused on maternal health and newborn babies, on cancer, tuber-culosis, venereal diseases, high blood pressure, cardiac care, diabetes, childhood diseases and other common physical infirmities. But now we saw new interest in the chronically mentally ill.

However, there was still a lot of work to be done for the acutely ill as well as teaching good health habits to the younger home-makers and their pre-schoolers. It was a challenge to take on the total approach to encourage stable and strong families with an emphasis on family togetherness.

These were functions in home visitations that I really enjoyed as a public health nurse. There was a great need to build family cohesion; to help families hold together against those pressures of migration which often created enormous family disruptions.

Most of the East Dayton residents I met were from rural parts of Kentucky or West Virginia, and like many immigrants before them, the complexities of life and work in a large city were often too much for them to bear. This, too, was an opportunity to work as a liaison person, bringing together medical services, social services and churches as well as other health and welfare agencies. I had the opportunity to contribute to a huge effort.

Working as a public health nurse in Ohio was not the same as in Wisconsin, where most of the patients I saw were older and belonged to some foreign ethnic group. In Wisconsin, most of my work consisted of bedside nursing care, instruction in food selection and preparation, and advice on better diets involving strange foods. There, the family structure was more stable.

But in Ohio, the families tended to be younger, less structured and often needing some sort of social support, guidance and continuous follow-up.

This is what made the work in Dayton a joy, and truly fulfilling. There was always the sense of accomplishment after helping improve the quality of life for the patients.

In my effort to provide these social and medical services, I learned that people, in the main, are wonderful. Most were glad to assist in the community work. If there was a need, regardless of what it was, the neighborhood responded and supported every request I made.

One such group was from St. Joseph's Catholic church. This all-male group asked me what they could do to improve life in the district, which at one time had been a heavily Catholic neighborhood. It was a heart-warming request. I immediately suggested food baskets for holidays such as Thanksgiving and Christmas.

Their response was wonderful. I sometimes was amused to think of this odd partnership between a group of well-to-do white Catholic businessmen and me, a colored Methodist nurse and health worker, serving a largely white, non-Catholic population. I'm sure they were amused at times, too.

But the partnership worked, and even in the racially tense times of the 1950s and 1960s, we never let such petty considerations as race, religion or gender stand in the way of providing food and care to the people of the district.

Then, after about four years of working together, they asked me if I knew of any needy colored families in my neighborhood. When they asked that, I knew these were truly concerned men who did not allow the differences among people overcome their similarities. Of course, I knew some needy colored people, and they were also helped.

I continued working as a public health nurse in District 10 until the early 1960s. I felt I had been of service in many areas of my field, but now I was interested in a new area: mental health.

Since public awareness and hard work by many health agencies had eliminated or controlled many health problems, I was restless and began looking for some new avenues of service. Mental health theory and practice attracted me. The need for rehabilitation and restoration in the chronic individual was one way I could help.

One such area is alcoholism, even though it was a field where little scientific knowledge was available at the time. I had interest, indeed great concern, in caring for the chronic drinker.

It was a time when one simply didn't talk very much about alcoholism, nor for that matter, of one's desire to work with alcoholics. Many of my co-workers thought I must have been an alcoholic. For the first few years I spent a lot of time defending myself.

I subscribed to some good magazines and collected current material on the care and treatment of alcoholics. I attended local and state conferences on the subject. Sometimes I was the only woman, or the only colored person, in attendance. But I read everything I could and talked to many alcohol-dependent people.

In 1964 the Surgeon General of the U. S. sent waves through American society when he reported for the first time that alcoholism was a disease and as such could be treated effectively. Until then it was most often regarded as a character flaw, something to be solved with pep talks or preaching.

Now the Surgeon General said it could be treated as other illnesses were treated. It gave health care professionals something to work for: the improved health of the chronic drinker.

In the summer of 1968 I was hired by the U. S. Government as a public health nurse-counselor. I would work as a staff member in a restoration facility located at the Veterans Medical Center in Dayton.

The program was a grass-roots concept with a new approach to chronic alcoholism. We were to treat it as a form of drug abuse. And the program was established to treat the patient as a whole person; this treatment included medical care, vocational training and social guidance. This was a new concept of care, and it required a greater knowledge of the total approach to care.

This work proved to be the most difficult of all the tasks I encountered during my entire nursing career. Yet it also was the most fascinating assignment I could have taken on.

The work brought me into contact with troubled persons and even those who had reached rock-bottom. Among them were veterans who had become withdrawn, suspicious and untidy. A particular one I recall walked with a limp, and became uncomfortable when I questioned him about his infirmity.

He said he had lost his big toe on his right foot. Thinking perhaps he had been injured on active duty, I pressed him for details and was shocked to learn he had lost his toe from frostbite while in a state of drunkenness.

Observng this man, and others like him, my feelings of compassion and concern made me realize that there were many veterans who needed help. But I lacked the proper training to work effectively with these persons.

I requested help to become better qualified to work with alcoholics. The U. S. Department of Health, Education and Welfare granted me unlimited training in one of the better schools studying alcoholism at that time, the Atlanta University School of Social Work.

I was home again.

The training was excellent, and I returned to my job feeling more knowledgeable and more confident, ready to work with chemically dependent people.

We immediately began to develop and implement what became one of the more accepted teaching programs of the early 1970s. Our concept was holistic and we even dealt with the bad effects of smoking, achieving excellent results in both areas.

The treatment used by our staff on the average patient was twofold. First, restore the patient's health and second, try to identify a reason or purpose for the patient to stay sober.

Much thought and work went into the effort, and much came out as a result of our planning. We restored some of the men; others we were unable to reach.

When my colleagues would despair over the difficulties of working with alcoholics, I would answer, "In long-term dependency, you win some and you lose some." Which was to say that some patients became sober, socially interactive and productive, even if some others made no attempt to change their habits.

For many who learned to live again it was a new chance at life. Many regained not only their general health but became productive citizens again. The response from families was tremendous.

When the program ended in 1979 after eleven busy years many of its concepts and practices were transferred to other departments and became the forerunner of concepts in use today.

When the program ended, I transferred to the drug addiction program newly started by the Ohio Department of Drug Abuse at the Project Cure treatment center in Dayton. The treatment center, like the alcoholism effort, combined medical services with counseling.

The clinic, under the direction of a physician, was open daily to dispense methadone, an artificial heroin substitute, to ease the withdrawal pains of addicts. The staff of Project Cure worked closely with other such clinics throughout the United States in ongoing medication, follow-up and support services.

I was glad to be able to make use of my previous training, experience and contacts in the alcohol abuse program. The aim of the therapist in both kinds of patient is total recovery from dependency.

My tour of duty with Project Care was to last for seven years.

In December, 1986 I felt it was time for me to reduce the speed and pace associated with full-time professional nursing.

After having been actively involved for more than eighteen years in the care and treatment of the chemically dependent — and for more than fifty years as a nurse totally committed to quality care for those in her charge — I felt it was time to retire from active nursing.

This didn't mean I was to separate myself from the needs of others. But I was now willing to step aside and rest, and do some of the other things I had always wanted to do for myself, including being a grandmother.

The activities I had put off included writing, cooking and traveling. I also wanted to work with the elderly, visit in nursing homes and with homebound persons. I also wanted to volunteer in the school system to work with disturbed children and to help where they might need me.

In those fifty-plus years of professional nursing, I had experienced many wonderful opportunities for study, for advancement, and for travel. I had overcome some formidable odds to meet and learn something about the people of the world.

It was these and other virtues that I found in my work, and the love for people, that enabled me to enjoy every day of my fifty years in nursing.

Retirement is anticipated with somewhat mixed emotions.

I had been busy for more than fifty years with daily activities as a nurse, counselor, care-giver, supporter and comforter to those under my care. There were no limits to my interest, devotion and caring for my patients.

Wherever there was a need, I had a solution. There were always agencies, organizations, churches and people of means to help. It was through these wonderful civic-minded people that I was able to provide help to the needy. I am grateful for the opportunity to serve.

In retrospect, it seemed like a long time. But when one stops to reminisce about the past, and its purpose and opportunities of service, one feels again the same strong desire to help. The goal of service had to be real to start with.

In remembering the good as well as the bad, the strong points and the weak points encountered during the busy years, there was never a moment or task when I didn't feel confident of ultimate success. Starting with my basic training in nursing, and throughout my entire fifty years as a nurse, I never gave a moment's thought to failure. Instead, I always thought of doing the best possible job of which I was capable, taking advantage of all the opportunities to learn and to put to use all the knowledge available. I can't give enough praise to my wonderful and caring parents, Oscar and Minnie Ivory, who set the example in our home for a life style to live and grow by. It was their early training, motivation, spiritual values and support that provided me with all the encouragement I needed to reach my goals.

The basic training and preparation given me as a student at Brewster School of Nursing was the best. The complete education I received opened the way for good employment as a professional nurse, at excellent salaries, in any of the states.

It gave me a chance to travel and meet many people, and to study the customs of foreigners, experiencing their interests and their feelings for Americans.

Now, with retirement, I look forward to more time to travel and to write, two of my most compelling interests.

CHAPTER ELEVEN

Return to Brewster

In June of 1987, following my retirement from active nursing, I returned to Brewster Hospital after almost fifty years of absence.

It was my first visit back to the school since that unforgettable day in 1941 when I boarded the train to start my Army service at Fort Bragg.

The beautiful scenery was no longer the way I recalled it on that day in September 1937 when I first arrived on campus. The bright red brick buildings were missing, too. Instead, there were new modern high-rise buildings — a new hospital.

I had expected changes, as I know nothing remains the same. But the memories of the magnificent flowers had remained engraved in my mind all those years.

Regardless, it was good to be coming back to the school that had made such a difference in my life. No matter what changes had come about, this was *Brewster*. This was the first reunion I had been able to attend. I had looked forward to the visit and seeing it all again. What a joy on arriving! There they were. The same four classmates who had greeted me on that memorable first day at Brewster fifty years ago, September 9, 1937:

Evelyn Jefferson-Hillman, now a licensed funeral home director in Jacksonville, Florida, mother of two children and a grandmother;

Annie Sue Martin-Brinson, founder and owner of a thriving business, the Victoria Martin Nursing Home in St. Petersburg, Florida;

Irene Parrish-Dowdell, who has enjoyed continuous hospital employment, later private duty nursing, and has been a tremendous force in the professional nursing community, and;

Ida Mae Trapp-Tyson, retired from the government's Veterans' Medical Center in Hampton, Virginia.

Visiting with these classmates and others made me very happy. We all were glad to make the return visit.

In recalling the old school and its advantages, but noting the new buildings, the additional bed space and the expanded services, we all approved of the progress. At the same time, we felt a profound closeness with and loyalty to the past. We realized we were a part of that past; that now we are a part of the present and a vital part of the future.

While it is fun to reminisce we cannot dwell in the past. Yes, we remember old Brewster as it was, but we support the new pace-setting Methodist Hospital which carries on its traditions of up-to-the-minute quality care of the ill. We pledge as Brewster graduates that we will forever be loyal and supportive of the old concepts but will grasp the new and progressive ideas of medical care. We embrace excellence in the nursing profession, and maintain the spiritual values which motivated us.

Although this was an outstanding achievement for the Methodist women and the colored nurses, Brewster Hospital and the nursing school were closed in 1967 when it was felt that the Church's mission to the black community had been accomplished.

The closing was due primarily to the fundamental changes taking place in American culture. The cost of providing medical care was rising, and the 1964 Civil Rights Act was removing racial barriers from other hospitals in the area.

The Women's Home Missionary Society, which had long battled racial discrimination, realized that the civil rights legislation was long overdue, and they favored it even though Brewster suffered financially.

The societal changes inspired them to devise a Master Development Plan which would carry Brewster Hospital and its services into the future with one of the most innovative health care facilities ever to open in Jacksonville.

Brewster Hospital's property was transferred to a new corporation named the Methodist Hospital and a fund drive was organized to build a major new health facility for the people of Jacksonville. Ground was broken in 1973 and the first phase of the new hospital was opened on June 29, 1975. Regarded as "The Miracle on Eighth

Street," the hospital has since grown tremendously and now is the principal health care provider in the North Jacksonville area.

To the many traditional services pioneered so long ago at Brewster were added the many new ones required by the times. Cancer detection, research, mental health, chemical dependencies, hospice care, geriatrics and child abuse services are but some of the new ways a great tradition continues to serve all the people of Jacksonville.

CHAPTER TWELVE

A Historical Look At Some Home Mission Work

In 1910 Bethlehem House was founded in Augusta, Georgia when Miss Mary de Bardeleben offered to work with Negroes. She was the daughter of a white Alabama Methodist minister, educated at Columbia Teachers College in New York and at Scarritt College, Nashville, Tennessee. The official opening of Bethlehem House finally occurred in 1912.

In 1913 Miss Estelle Haskins and other faculty members of the Scarritt Methodist Training School in Nashville became interested in Negro settlement work.

Their continuing efforts were used by the social science department at Fisk University in Nashville as a demonstration center. This was the first and finest example of interracial cooperation on a grand basis, thanks to that first appeal for help from black women. Other outstanding efforts included the Friendship Community Clubs, welcoming participation from black and white residents of many communities.

The Interdenominational Commission on Interracial Cooperation, headquartered in Atlanta, encouraged local groups to help promote racial cooperation. Their aim was to remove causes of friction between the races in southern communities, where racial antagonism reigned.

Atlanta today may be reaping some of the good that the Methodist women established in the early years of their Home Missions in Christianity. It is a thriving metropolitan city, living in racial harmony, one of the most progressive cities of the south with several outstanding Negro colleges and universities which work well with white institutions. Surely the spirit of these Methodist women still prevails in this great southern city.

In the late 19th century southern Methodist women were discovering new opportunities for service in home missions, and the churches' work was a respectable outlet for women's energies. As Lucinda Helm reviewed those years, she could find satisfaction amid the difficulties.

She noted one Bishop Hargrove had made the call, "and women, brave and true, had responded with the loving zeal that only a woman's heart can know. Contending against obstacles unexpected, battling against indifference where we ought to find ready responses, soothing the jealousy of mistaken zealots for other organizations, but ever guided and helped by God, we have gone forward slowly in regard to numbers, but we have accomplished a great work."

Taking their cues from advocates of social Christianity, the women stressed the importance of extending Christ's kingdom on earth.

During more than half a century of home mission work, the women's efforts were diverse and far-reaching. They showed particular concern for home structure, especially the well-being of children. They supported Prohibition, counseled moral strictness, sought social improvements and updated medical care for those living in poverty.

A close examination of their work shows that religious ideas, especially the vision of extending the kingdom of God on earth, were a major factor in instigating and shaping their varied reform activities.

One of the early leaders was Ohioan Lucy Hayes, wife of President Rutherford B. Hayes. Following the 1880 General Conference in Cincinnati, home missions rapidly expanded. The group was then known as the Women's Home Missionary Society of the Methodist Episcopal Church, and in 1883 established seven Bureaus of Information to obtain facts about problems and to make suggestions on solutions.

Two such bureaus in the south included one for colored people and another for illiterate whites. Throughout the last years of the century they promoted training for women in homemaking and other vocational skills, as well as religious and moral training.

As early as 1830 Mrs. M. L. Kelley, wife of a Methodist minister, established a society at one of the churches on the Lebanon circuit in Bethlehem, Tennessee. Later, in 1850, she rejuvenated the work to support mission efforts of Mr. and Mrs. J. W. Lambuth in Shanghai, China.

The Civil War ended this effort but Mrs. Kelley would not be thwarted. In the early 1870s she again attempted to organize a missionary society in McKendree Church in Nashville, where her son was the pastor.

Her purpose was to serve not only foreign missions but also to visit the sick and aid the poor while instructing them in the scriptures. Another of her major home missions was to assist in the founding of a home for unwed mothers.

The blossoming interest in mission work among southern Methodist women led eventually, in 1878, to the founding of the Women's Board of Foreign Missions by the General Conference of the church.

Four years later, in 1882, Dr. T. R. Kendall formed the Trinity Home Mission in Atlanta. At Trinity most of the work was done with black women and children and combined social and religious elements: sewing classes were followed by Bible lessons.

With a broadened authority, the southern Methodist women undertook a range of home mission activities. The response was quick. Education for the poor and the unchurched came fast.

In 1892 the Wolf Mission School was opened in Ybor City, Florida for the children of Cuban immigrants. A similar project followed two years later in Tampa.

In 1896 the Sue Bennett Memorial School was founded in London, Kentucky for the poor children of that area, Later that year the Industrial Home at Greeneville, Tennessee opened for orphans.

In 1894 the Central Committee approved a course of reading material pertinent to home mission work, and announced it in the *Our Homes* publication. Lily Hammond, daughter of a slave owner and a prolific writer, argued that if America was to remain a Christian nation, "Americans must better understand their country – its needs, its perils, its resources, as well as the work which other Christian people are doing in this and other lands for the cause at heart!"

Mrs. Hammond, wife of the white president of black Paine College, was convinced that lack of education was the greatest stumbling block to social reform.

"We want to know of everything," she wrote, "that is being done in all the world to uplift the fallen, to better the condition of the poor, to bring classes together, to make straight paths for stumbling feet, whether the work be for physical, mental or spiritual betterment of those who are in need."

In 1921 Will Alexander, long active in and supportive of the Home Missions, wrote to a friend also involved in mission activities that, "the women's missionary council of the ME Church, South was the most progressive and constructive religious group in the South."

Certainly the opposition that the women encountered in advocating home missions was, to a significant degree, in the perception people held of women's proper role in society. The women's struggle to expand that role within their denominations highlights the opposition they faced in more than a half century of work.

When the Louisiana Conference met in 1881, it was announced that the auxiliary was working under severe disadvantage at Litchfield, Kentucky. When asked what the difficulties were, the chorused reply was "Husbands!"

In 1902 the women founded Brewster Hospital in Jacksonville, Florida for the care of colored patients. One of the first schools for training colored nurses was opened as part of the hospital. Brewster Hospital and its training school for nurses lasted until 1967 when it became the base for the brand new and much larger Methodist Hospital.

Primary Sources

Anderson, Carolyn M., *United Methodists - Black Methodists For Church Renewal*, Dayton, Ohio, 1990.

Brummitt, Stella Wyatt, *Looking Backward, Thinking Forward*, The Jubilee History of the Women's Home Missionary Society of the Methodist Episcopal Church, Cincinnati, Ohio, 1930.

Cannon, James, III, *History of Southern Methodist Missions*, Methodist Publishing House, Nashville, Tennessee, 1926.

McDowell, John Patrick, *The Social Gospel In The South, The Women's Home Mission Movement in the Methodist Episcopal Church, South, 1886-1939*, Louisiana State University Press, 1982.

The author shortly before her retirement.